Praise for *The New Leadership Literacies*

"For leaders of the future everywhere, this is a vitally important book to prepare us all for a world where all can thrive."
—Chris Ernst, Global Head, Leadership and Organization Development, Bill & Melinda Gates Foundation, and coauthor of *Boundary Spanning Leadership*

"Bob Johansen is out in front of us again. In this book, Bob gives fair warning and great developmental guidance for those of us who aspire to lead into the future."
—Bob Anderson, CEO, and Bill Adams, Chairman and Chief Development Officer, The Leadership Circle, and authors of *Mastering Leadership*

"This book will be an important point of reference for what we all need to take into account as we try to find our place in the perpetually changing new world, and it will be especially relevant to those who will try to lead us in that world."
—Edgar H. Schein, Professor Emeritus, MIT Sloan School of Management, and author of *Humble Inquiry* and *Humble Consulting*

"I oversee talent for the San Francisco Giants. Bob's book provides new literacies to help discover and nurture the next championship talent to be team leaders."
—John Barr, Vice President and Assistant General Manager, San Francisco Giants

"To understand the gift that is Bob Johansen and *The New Leadership Literacies*, imagine twenty top CEOs in a workshop sharing their volatile, uncertain, complex, and ambiguous angst. Foresight yields to insight, which portends action. Hope is renewed. It is powerful and humbling. Years after Bob spoke to our roundtable, his concepts are still discussed at every meeting."
—Brenda C. Curiel, Managing Director, CCI, Inc.

"I will be using this book in my Give.org work, and I urge others striving to produce social good to do so as well."
—H. Art Taylor, President and CEO, BBB Wise Giving Alliance

"Now, as executive director of FRED Leadership, I plan to use Bob and *The New Leadership Literacies* to further the thinking on this critical topic with top leadership/executive development programs."
—David Small, Executive Director, FRED Leadership

"Bob's new book once again pushes me out of my comfort zone—but it helps me imagine what it will take to thrive in a future of extreme disruption."
—Carmen M. Allison, Vice President, Talent, Pottery Barn Brands and Global Talent Development, Williams-Sonoma, Inc.

"This book offers thoughtful and practical literacies for leading rather than react-ing. Our graduate students as well as our program partners in faith communities, social innovation, and values-based companies will learn ways to turn fear and uncertainty into vision and opportunity."

—David Vásquez-Levy, President, Pacific School of Religion

"*The New Leadership Literacies* is the perfect deep dive into preparing to thrive in this increasingly uncertain world."

—Kathy Mandato, Vice President, Human Resources, Snap, Inc.

"Bob is a master in making sense of what leaders will need to survive disruptive blasts from the future. We are aggressively using Bob's new literacies for immer-sive executive development."

—Jack McCarthy, Director, Executive Development Roundtable, and Associate Professor of Organizational Behavior, Questrom School of Business, Boston University

"I will personally use *The New Leadership Literacies* in my work at CCL to guide decisions about research we will undertake and how our solutions will develop leaders who are "future literate."

—Jennifer W. Martineau, Senior Vice President, Research, Evaluation, and Societal Advancement, Center for Creative Leadership

"Bob's leadership literacies are a natural and welcomed complement to our pro-grams, in which we immerse executives in the leadership lessons from West Point and the US Army."

—Karen Kuhla, Executive Director, Thayer Leader Development Group

"In my role with the Foresight Council, I will be using the ideas in this book to guide corporate foresight leaders as they help shape the future."

—Rick Holman, Director, Foresight Council, and past leader, GM Global Foresight Network

"Bob Johansen invites each generation to live on the edge of their competencies to read the future backward and grasp hold of the signs that beckon us forward. He invites us to transcend what we don't know with honesty. In so doing, he knows we will create curious leaders and curious communities who will resist the urge to freak out and instead leapfrog into our new awaiting future. Though we all face a dilemma-ridden world, Johansen offers *The New Leadership Literacies* to collab-oratively hack the outskirts of a hope that awaits us."

—C. Andrew Doyle, IX Episcopal Bishop, Diocese of Texas

"Bob's work has been critical to developing our leaders to think in new ways and support an innovative culture. We are using *The New Leadership Literacies* to help develop visionary leadership."

—Leah Toney Podratz, Director, Organization Development, Cox Enterprises

THE NEW LEADERSHIP LITERACIES

THE NEW
LEADERSHIP
LITERACIES

Thriving
in a Future of
Extreme Disruption
and Distributed
Everything

BOB
JOHANSEN

Institute for the Future

Berrett-Koehler Publishers, Inc.
a BK Business book

Berrett-Koehler Publishers, Inc.
1333 Broadway, Suite 1000
Oakland, CA 94612-1921
Tel: (510) 817-2277   Fax: (510) 817-2278
www.bkconnection.com

All figures, unless otherwise indicated, © 2016 Institute for the Future. All rights reserved.
SR-1908 | www.iftf.org

ORDERING INFORMATION
Quantity sales. Special discounts are available on quantity purchases by corporations, associations, and others. For details, contact the "Special Sales Department" at the Berrett-Koehler address above.
Individual sales. Berrett-Koehler publications are available through most bookstores. They can also be ordered directly from Berrett-Koehler: Tel: (800) 929-2929; Fax: (802) 864-7626; www.bkconnection.com
Orders for college textbook/course adoption use. Please contact Berrett-Koehler: Tel: (800) 929-2929; Fax: (802) 864-7626.

Distributed to the U.S. trade and internationally by Penguin Random House Publisher Services.

Berrett-Koehler and the BK logo are registered trademarks of Berrett-Koehler Publishers, Inc.

Printed in Canada

Berrett-Koehler books are printed on long-lasting acid-free paper. When it is available, we choose paper that has been manufactured by environmentally responsible processes. These may include using trees grown in sustainable forests, incorporating recycled paper, minimizing chlorine in bleaching, or recycling the energy produced at the paper mill.

Library of Congress Cataloging-in-Publication Data
Names: Johansen, Robert, author.
Title: The new leadership literacies : thriving in a future of extreme disruption and distributed everything / Bob Johansen.
Description: First edition. | Oakland, California : Berrett-Koehler Publishers, [2017] | Includes bibliographical references.
Identifiers: LCCN 2017012329 | ISBN 9781626569614 (hardcover)
Subjects: LCSH: Leadership. | Organizational change.
Classification: LCC HD57.7 .J6353 2017 | DDC 658.4/092—dc23
LC record available at https://lccn.loc.gov/2017012329

FIRST EDITION
22 21 20 19 18 17 | 10 9 8 7 6 5 4 3 2

Produced by BookMatters, copyedited by Tanya Grove, proofed by Janet Reed Blake, indexed by Leonard Rosenbaum. Jacket design by Archie Ferguson. Jacket illustration by Kent Kuhn, Institute for the Future.

To our children and grandchildren,
who call me to the future

CONTENTS

PREFACE

We think we are connected today, but the next ten years will be a period of explosive connectivity and asymmetric upheaval. In this future world of dramatically amplified digital connectivity, anything that can be distributed will be distributed. Most leaders—and most organizations—aren't ready for this future.

We are on a twisting path toward—but never quite reaching—a place where everything will be distributed. This path will be characterized by increasing speed, frequency, scope, and scale of disruption.

Younger leaders will be better prepared for this future than older leaders. Many young people are in a blended-reality world already with constant mobile online filters for the physical world. They are on online, unless they are off. For most adult leaders, we are offline—unless we are on. Quaintly, some leaders today still say they "log on" to the internet. And do we really need to capitalize the word *internet* any longer? I think not, and this is the first book I've written where I'm not capitalizing the word *internet*. It is pervasive already, but this is just the beginning.

Leadership will be much less centralized and much more distributed in this future. The hierarchical practices of leadership for centralized organizations will be brittle in a future world that is not only decentralized but also distributed. Firm structures will give way to shape-shifting organizational forms that function like organisms. Enduring leadership qualities like strength, humility, and trust will still be foundational, but the future will require new literacies for leading.

It's too late to catch up, but it's a great time to leapfrog. I introduce in this book five ways for current and future leaders to take their own leap to the future.

- **Learn to look backward from the future.** The future will reward clarity—but punish certainty. Looking long will help differentiate between the waves of change that can be ridden and those that must be avoided. Judging too soon will be dangerous, but deciding too late will be even worse.

- **Voluntarily engage in fear.** Think of this as gaming for grit, creating readiness for an increasingly frightening and unpredictable world. Again, the kids will have a competitive advantage since many of them have grown up playing video games. I believe that gaming—emotionally laden first-person stories—will evolve into the most powerful learning medium in history. Most kids will be ready for this world; most adults will not.

- **Embrace shape-shifting organizations.** New organizational forms will become possible through distributed computing networks, which have no center, grow from the edges, and will be uncontrollable. Hierarchies will come and go, as they are needed. Economies of scale (where bigger is almost always better) will give way to economies of organizational structure, in which you are what you can organize. Authority will be much more distributed. Fluid shape-shifting organizations will win consistently over centralized hierarchies. Disturbingly, terrorists and criminals already make use of shape-shifting organizations better than most of the rest of us.

- **Be there even when you're not there.** Most of today's leaders are best in person, but they will not be able to be there in person all the time. Their ability to lead will be reduced dramatically if they cannot continuously *feel* present even when they are not present. New digital tools will allow leaders to bridge the valley created by their absence in ways that move beyond being there. The best leaders will be close—but not too close—even when they are at a distance.

- **Create and sustain positive energy.** Leaders will need to radiate positive energy at all times, and that will require them to have physical, mental, and spiritual well-being. In this highly uncertain future, hope will be the key variable—particularly for young people. Young people who are hopeful and digitally connected will be inspiring. Young people who are hopeless and digitally connected will be dangerous. Leaders will need to seed realistic hope in a future that will be laced with fear.

I'm asking you as leaders to understand and practice these new leadership literacies, but also to open yourself to new leadership literacies, new practices for engaging with an increasingly uncertain world.

For at least the next decade, the world will be in a scramble: many things that have been stuck will become unstuck. A scramble is a ripe time for innovation, and leaders will see things they've never seen before. The new leadership literacies will provide a process for taking advantage of the scramble, enabling leaders to make the future in positive and practical ways.

The intended audiences for this book include

- **Current, rising star, and aspiring leaders**—of all ages—especially leaders who wonder about their readiness for the future. This book is a great pre-read before a leadership team retreat or conference on the future, for example. It also makes a great end-of-year gift to get people thinking about the future in creative ways. Boards of directors and top leadership teams will use this book to help them think about the future of their own organizations.

- **Human resources leaders** and others looking to hire leaders who will thrive in the world of the future. Anyone seeking to develop a talent profile for the future will find a rich collection of resources here. Before you post your next job description, read this book.

- **Innovation and organizational design leaders** who are imagining new ways to lead.

- **Designers and leaders of development programs** of any length. This book would be an excellent tool for those who are preparing leaders for external future forces, as it provides guidelines for imagining new approaches that will help leaders get ready for the future.

- **Executive coaches** seeking a fresh view of the future, who will be exploring how leaders will need to prepare. This book shows just what kind of coaching will work best, given the external future forces of the next decade.

The core of this book is five pairs of chapters, one pair for each future leadership literacy. The first chapter in each pair defines the literacy and how it differs from current leadership practices. The second chapter in each pair probes the future we are moving toward with that literacy.

The Table of Contents is a good overview, and you can read the chapters in any order—depending on your interests and priorities. My big-picture forecast (twisting toward distributed everything) introduces the book and it is a great place to start to get the gist of the future that leaders will be facing. I end the book with a call to action, a practical and future-oriented guide to leading with realistic hope.

This book is grounded in foresight. By looking ten or more years ahead and then coming back, leaders can see the subtle patterns of change that are not visible in the noisy present. My goal is to use my foresight to provoke your insight and your action. There is short-term value to long-term thinking.

My publisher, Berrett-Koehler, has created a companion product to this book: an online future readiness self-assessment (see link in the back of this book). This self-assessment includes the five future leadership literacies and the ten future leadership skills from my earlier book *Leaders Make the Future*, as well as advice for how to improve in each area. I suggest setting a goal for yourself one year from now. You can take the self-assessment up to five times over the next year. It is a great conversation starter for your own leadership development or for group experiences with your team. I will be using it before, during, and after my talks and workshops.

INTRODUCTION

Twisting Toward
Distributed Everything

THE SHIFT FROM CENTRALIZED TO DISTRIBUTED ORGA-
nizations has already begun, but the current leadership literacy—inherited
from large centralized organizations—isn't ready for a future when anything that can be distributed will be distributed.

Centralized and decentralized organizations will give way to truly distributed organizations that have no center, grow from the edges, and cannot
be controlled. Hierarchies will come and go in shape-shifting forms resem-
bling a swirl. Rock-star leaders will be rare; networked leadership with
strength and humility will work best. As centralized organizations become
increasingly distributed, expect a cloudburst of disruption. In this future,
leaders will see things they have never seen before.

My hope is that readers will allow themselves to be provoked by this
book. It doesn't really matter if you agree with my forecasts or not; it matters
only if they provoke you in useful ways. In fact, some of the best forecasts
are those you don't like—forecasts that cause you to think and do things you
would not have done otherwise.

This book will suggest a process for developing your own future leader-

1

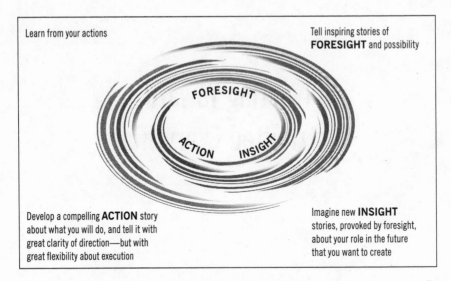

Learn from your actions

Tell inspiring stories of **FORESIGHT** and possibility

FORESIGHT

ACTION   INSIGHT

Develop a compelling **ACTION** story about what you will do, and tell it with great clarity of direction—but with great flexibility about execution

Imagine new **INSIGHT** stories, provoked by foresight, about your role in the future that you want to create

FIGURE 1 In the future, leaders will have to practice foresight, insight, and action.

ship literacies, a process that will cycle from foresight to insight to action— in a continuous and bidirectional flow (see Figure 1).

In simpler times, perhaps being action oriented was enough to make a great leader. Perhaps the future was clearer back then, the insights more obvious. In the past, consultants and business books preached *action* as the defining characteristic of great leaders. But even thousands of hours of action experience won't be enough for this future. Leaders will need to develop new literacies in new ways for new futures. Action will not be enough to win in the kind of future that is emerging. Action without foresight and insight will be dumb, dangerous, or both. Leaders will need to combine the practices of foresight, insight, and action in an ongoing cycle of learning.

The next decade will be extremely complex, messy, and threatening. Future leaders will be facing a VUCA world: Volatile, Uncertain, Complex, and Ambiguous. I learned this term at the Army War College in Carlisle, Pennsylvania, where I have done immersion experiences, workshops, and talks since 9/11. This book is about what's next in what I believe will be an increasingly VUCA world, a pothole-filled path winding toward—but never quite reaching—a future when everything is distributed.

The word that best characterizes the near future is *scramble*: lots of things that have been stuck will get unstuck. In the ensuing scramble, many creative things will happen—including shifts that are very different from what the scramblers intended. Those who are good at unsticking—the scramblers—are not likely to be very good at putting things back together again in new ways. This is a future that will be full of innovation that can be put to all kinds of uses—for good and for evil.

I'll be using the Foresight-Insight-Action Cycle to summarize how leaders can develop their own personal process of leading in the midst of the scramble.

In Future Tense

In this book, I explore the external future forces most likely to disrupt leaders, give practical advice for how they can make the future a better place, and suggest an ideal talent profile for future leaders. *The New Leadership Literacies* has many signals from the future, but there are no facts about the future.

I propose five new leadership literacies, but I ask that you open yourself to others that go beyond what I am suggesting. The literacies I introduce here will give you a head start on the future, but there will be others to come. What we've been taught about leadership in the past won't be enough—even though each new literacy should be informed by enduring leadership wisdom from the past.

My views are based on working as a professional futurist in Silicon Valley for some forty years. My forecasts are plausible, internally consistent, and provocative. While nobody can predict the future, my forecast futures over the years have usually happened. While I don't claim to be an expert in the present, I have been pretty good at listening for and foreseeing the future. The best futurists I know don't quite fit in the present. I don't quite fit in the present either, and I think that is an advantage.

In 1973, Institute for the Future had new grants from the National Science Foundation (NSF) and Advanced Research Projects Agency (now called DARPA) to study the use of the emerging network for communication among scientists in the early 1970s, and I was able to join them shortly after that and come to Silicon Valley. It was clear to me by then that being a professor of sociology was not my calling; I was—and still am—called by the future.

Institute for the Future (IFTF) was a spin-off of RAND Corporation and Stanford Research Institute (now called SRI International) in 1968. IFTF is one of the few futures research groups in the world that has outlived its forecasts. We look back every ten years and ask how we've done. Over those forty-plus years, 60 to 80 percent of our forecast futures have actually happened, depending on your definition of *happened*. Even though we're usually right, we don't use the word *predict*. Nobody can predict the future. I like to say, "If somebody tells you they can predict the future, you shouldn't believe them . . . especially if they're from California." The goal of looking out ten years is to look backward from the future and provoke, not predict.

When I came to Silicon Valley and joined Institute for the Future, I was hired to help prototype and evaluate what today would be called social media for scientists communicating with other scientists at NASA, USGS, NSF, defense contractor universities, and other government agencies—since those were the only people who could use what we now call the internet. Instead of *social media*, we used the nerdy name *computer conferencing* to describe these media, and our prototype system was called Forum. Jacques Vallee was leading our team at IFTF, and I was leading the evaluation research on these early forms of social media. This was more than ten years before The Well, which was arguably the first social medium for wider populations. We were prototyping social media, but only defense contractors could use our system since they were the only people allowed on the ARPANET at the time.

I have a vivid memory of getting a frantic call one morning from a staff person in a general's office at the Pentagon. To the staffer's urgent disgust, his general had just received a personal message directly through our system from a lowly research assistant at a defense contractor university. The message sent via Forum to the general was a biting complaint about the Vietnam War, as I recall. The general's assistant shouted at me in horror: "Do you mean that just anybody can now send a crazy message directly to my general?"

"Uh, yes sir . . . at least anyone on our network," I replied sheepishly. The twisting path toward a future when everything is distributed had cracked open just a bit. The move toward distributed authority was just getting going.

Much later in 2016 at Nestlé, the world's largest food company, the Salesforce Chatter internal social media platform is being used to promote internal communication across a radically distributed organization. Chris Johnson, the executive in charge of Nestlé Business Excellence and one of the top executives in this very large organization, said recently: "I love interacting with people across organizations without the barriers of hierarchy" (quoted in Blackshaw 2016). The VUCA world is accelerating.

The Positive VUCA

As I've worked with the VUCA world concept in a variety of organizations since 9/11, I've come to understand that it does have a hopeful side: volatility yields to vision; uncertainty to understanding; complexity to clarity; and ambiguity to agility.* Vision, understanding, clarity, and agility are foundational to the new leadership literacies that I am proposing in this book.

Inspired by my experiences at the Army War College, I wrote a book called *Leaders Make the Future* that focused on future leadership skills. That book is now in its second edition, and I'm convinced that the ten leadership skills I identified there are basic to successful leadership in the future: the maker instinct, clarity, dilemma flipping, constructive depolarizing, immersive learning ability, bio-empathy, quiet transparency, smart-mob organization, rapid prototyping, and commons creating.

Skills, however, won't be enough to thrive in the future world that is emerging. A single leadership literacy won't be enough either. Leaders will need to be multiliterate in this future world, just as international leaders are much stronger if they are multilingual. Leadership skills will have to be wrapped in broader literacies that combine:

- discipline, to provide order—but not too much order
- practices, to understand and share what works—and what doesn't

---

* I talk in much more detail about both the threats and the opportunities of the VUCA world in *The Reciprocity Advantage* and *Leaders Make the Future*.

- perspective, to learn from a wide diversity of views—but not get stuck in any single view
- worldview, to look long instinctively—but focus on action when that is needed

After introducing each new leadership literacy, I link it back to the skills I identified in *Leaders Make the Future*. This new book starts where *Leaders Make the Future* ended. You don't have to read *Leaders Make the Future* to get benefit from this book, but it will certainly add context, history, and depth. I hope that these two books will be used together for leadership development.

Leaders are—and must continue to be—a source of clarity. Clarity is the ability to be very explicit about where you are going, but very flexible about how you will get there.

In a future loaded with dilemmas, disruption will be rampant, and clarity will be scarce. The disruptions of the next decade will be beyond what many people can cope with. Many will be susceptible to simplistic solutions—especially from politicians and religions. Leaders will need to provide enough clarity to make disruption tolerable and even motivational. They will also need to communicate realistic hope through their own stories of clarity. Certainty about the future may provide temporary hope, but it is likely to be false hope since we live in an increasingly VUCA world.

VUCA has always been a part of life, beginning from the fact that we all have to die. Leaders have been challenged by VUCA before—but never on the global scale that they will experience over the next decade. My big three global VUCA challenges are global climate disruption, cyber terrorism, and pandemics—all of which will likely be on a scale that was previously unimaginable. VUCA has never before been so global, so interconnected, and so scalable. Local VUCA is not new; the VUCA *world* is unprecedented.

In the future, disruption will become the norm for most people, as the scope, frequency, nature, and impact of disruption explodes. Deep disruption will take a long time—often decades—to unfold.

As mentioned before, this book is divided into five pairs of chapters, each pair focusing on a future leadership literacy that leaders will need in order to thrive. For each new leadership literacy, I provide a chapter defining it

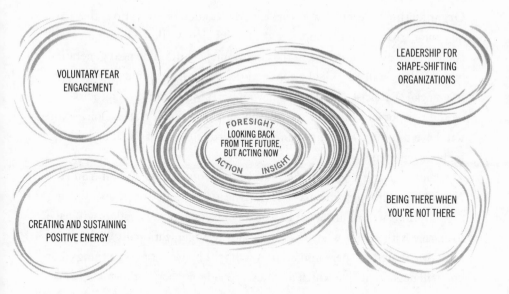

VOLUNTARY FEAR
ENGAGEMENT

LEADERSHIP FOR
SHAPE-SHIFTING
ORGANIZATIONS

FORESIGHT
LOOKING BACK
FROM THE FUTURE,
BUT ACTING NOW
ACTION   INSIGHT

BEING THERE WHEN
YOU'RE NOT THERE

CREATING AND SUSTAINING
POSITIVE ENERGY

FIGURE 2 The New Leadership Literacies

and a companion chapter with my forecast for the future of that literacy. I begin each forecast with a surprise.

Figure 2 is a visual overview of the book.

Here is the core structure and content.

Chapters 1 and 2 look at the literacy I call **Looking Backward from the Future**, which is about learning how to go out to the future (usually ten years out) and then work your way back. It will help you see the direction of change so that you can avoid the noise of the present and develop your clarity. To lead, you will need to be clear about direction (clarity will be rewarded) but flexible about execution (certainty will be punished).

Chapters 3 and 4 look at the literacy of **Voluntary Fear Engagement**, which is about gamefully engaging with your own fears in low-risk simulated worlds. Because next-generation disruption will be so dangerous and difficult to understand, safe zones will be needed where you can immerse yourself in fear and figure out how to succeed. Practice and learn with others, the way the military conducts war gaming. Then come back better prepared for the real thing.

Chapters 5 and 6 look at the literacy of **Leadership for Shape-Shifting**

Organizations. Learn how to thrive in distributed organizations that have no center, grow from the edges, and cannot be controlled. Hierarchies will come and go as needs arise and the environment shifts. The next generation of technology will provide the connective cord for distributed organizations so you can share risk and develop new opportunities. Since reciprocity will be the currency of this new world—not just traditional transactions—you will have to practice mutual-benefit partnering. Authority will be increasingly distributed.

Chapters 7 and 8 look at the literacy of **Being There When You Are Not There**. Although you may currently lead best in person, shape-shifting organizations will require you to be many places at once. Leaders will have to engage with people who are geographically, organizationally, and temporally distributed. In-person meetings will still be best for some things, but you will need to decide which medium is good for what, with which people, at what time.

Chapters 9 and 10 look at the literacy of **Creating and Sustaining Positive Energy**. You must regulate your personal energy so you have focus, stamina, and resilience when you need it. The VUCA world will be exhausting for everyone—but especially for leaders. You will have to be extremely fit, physically and psychologically—much more so than leaders in the past. And you will need spiritual (though not necessarily religious) grounding and a sense of meaning in the midst of extreme disruption.

"Distributed Everything" Started in Silicon Valley

When I first arrived in Silicon Valley, Institute for the Future was up in the hills on Sand Hill Road in Menlo Park, near Highway 280, barely on the inland side of the San Andreas Fault. I used to joke that, when The Big One hits California, Institute for the Future will have a shoreline view.

IFTF was the first tenant in a new cluster of buildings built by Tom Ford, a former development officer from Stanford, who had the foresight to buy a parcel of land right across the road from Stanford University property. He attracted a new kind of tenant in addition to our little think tank—people who would come to be called venture capitalists. Ford Land Company became a big success, venture capital boomed, and Sand Hill Road is now known as the Wall Street of Silicon Valley.

The Silicon Valley "Wall Street" is beauty on the edge of disaster. Droughts, wildfires, and mudslides loom. And earthquakes are omnipresent here—not only the geological kind but also metaphorical earthquakes of innovation.

I believe that the everyday juxtaposition of awesome beauty and certain disruption is an important reason why Silicon Valley is the birthplace of so much innovation—including the technologies pushing us toward distributed everything. The inevitability that our beautiful world will be disrupted is at least a partial motivator for all of us to innovate.

Silicon Valley disruptors have bloomed, seeded, re-bloomed, and re-seeded in continuing harvests of innovation—all under the certainty of disaster. If you live in a time when each day could be the eve of destruction, having the innovation jimjams is just part of your daily life. In other parts of the world, it may seem easier to fend off outside forces and maintain control through centralized organizations. But if you live in Silicon Valley, distributed everything just seems like what we all need to learn how to do. *Distributed* means dispersed over space and time. The technologies of dispersion have their roots here in Silicon Valley. Digital connectivity can link scattered people and processes, but it takes special human effort to weave new organizational forms, new business models, and new styles of leadership.

If the many colorful visions of how to improve the world were not so compelling and credible, Silicon Valley would never work. Silicon Valley has already changed the world, and there is strong reason to believe that it will do so again and again. It is the spirit of Silicon Valley that will make distributed everything possible.

There are two very powerful and very distributed clusters of disruptors in Silicon Valley: one obsessed with ways to make the world a better place, the other obsessed by extreme greed. These two loose social networks, whose members have compatible values, don't particularly like each other, but the world changers and the greedy people know they need each other. And there are some crossovers.

You may have negative associations with the word *greed*, but if it weren't for greed, Silicon Valley would not be the success story that it is. Tense relations between the world changers and impatient investors create friction,

FIGURE 3 Silicon Valley companies are paranoid about disruption. The two-sided sign at Facebook is a constant reminder for Facebook employees that nothing in Silicon Valley is permanent.

which sparks the innovators among them to throw hundreds of matches every day on bonfires of disruption.

Fail early, fail often, and fail cheaply is the motto here. Failure is a badge of courage. Success builds on earlier failures. Very little happens in Silicon Valley any more that is truly new. Almost everything that succeeds here was tried and failed many times before. "Our purpose is to fail, but to fail in an interesting way," said Silicon Valley visionary Alan Kay when he was at Xerox PARC during its prime. Failure is an essential ingredient of disruption, and Silicon Valley is full of people who thrive on disrupting in a climate of perpetual disruption.

The photo on the left side of Figure 3 is the sign as you drive onto the current (relatively new) Facebook campus in Menlo Park, just off Highway 101. The photo on the right is the back of the sign that Facebook retained from Sun Microsystems, which used to occupy the same campus. When Sun was still an independent company, its executives boasted that they expected to be disrupted, were fully prepared for disruption, and that they knew how to "eat [their] own young" in order to survive disruption. In spite of their efforts, Sun Microsystems was eaten by Oracle. The two-sided sign at Facebook is a constant reminder for Facebook employees that nothing in Silicon Valley is permanent. Disruption looms here.

Many books and most corporations focus on *trends*, which have data, duration, and direction. In the futures field, trends are patterns of change from which you can extrapolate with confidence. Demographic trends (for example, around aging or population flows) are important to track and anticipate, but trends are much easier to identify and follow than disruptions. With trends, you have historical data that is worthy of trust, so you have a pretty good sense of what's coming next. With disruptions, you have only hints about what's next, and the hints are often wrong.

Trends are gradual, relatively predictable, and almost-comfortable change. Disruption is extreme and unpredictable change. Disruption is uncomfortable for most people.

This book focuses on *disruptions*, which are *breaks* in the patterns of change. Disruptions tend to take a long time to play out and are often characterized by waves of innovation.

Disruptions often start as responses to particular problems but almost always spark unexpected changes. Despite its sense of immediacy, disruption is often a process that takes a long while to play out—disruption doesn't just suddenly pop up and then disappear.

When disruption first breaks out, it is hard to tell just what the core disruption will be. Early waves of disruption may look much different from what happens later.

Most people in today's organizations are not prepared for a global future laced with disruption and extreme dilemmas that have no easy answers. As former UK Prime Minister Tony Blair said right after the vote for Britain to leave the European Union in 2016:

> The political center has lost its power to persuade and its essential means of connection to the people it seeks to represent. Instead, we are seeing a convergence of the far left and far right. The right attacks immigrants while the left rails at bankers, but the spirit of insurgency, the venting of anger at those in power and the addiction to simple, demagogic answers to complex problems are the same for both extremes. Underlying it all is a shared hostility to globalization. (Blair 2016)

Despite the trendy "shared hostility to globalization," top leaders will deal mostly with dilemmas that are increasingly global and flow across national boundaries. Dilemmas are problems you can't solve, problems that won't go away—yet somehow leaders must learn how to succeed anyway. Future dilemmas will be embedded with both hope and fear—but the fear will be biting and the hope elusive.

If a leader characterizes a dilemma as a problem that can be solved, the failure to solve it is likely be remembered and probably will be punished. When dealing with extreme dilemmas, leaders will need to learn how to thrive in the space between judging too soon (the classic mistake of the problem solver) and deciding too late (the classic mistake of the academic). Dilemmas are gnarly.

The word *disruption* is out of fashion, I was told more than once as I was writing this book. Some friends suggested that I stop using the word, since it has been used in such cavalier ways recently. Even in Silicon Valley, a constant churn of jargon-laden innovation-speak, the word *disruption* has been overused and under-defined. Zoé Bezpalko, a young Silicon Valley friend of mine born in France, said to me with a twinkle in her eye: "Oh, haven't you heard? Disruption is now passé. Now, it's all about *invention*."

I kind of like that shift—and I certainly like the word *invention*—but I don't want to give up on the word *disruption*. Instead, I want to make it clear that I'm using the word *correctly* to mean a break in the patterns of change. In this book, I'm talking about really serious breaks in the patterns of change—beyond trends and the watered-down pop definition of *disruption*. Leaders will need to face up to disruption, not just call it by another name.

How can leaders learn not only to cope in the VUCA world but also thrive? The leadership literacies I am proposing will actually work *better* when the world is volatile, uncertain, complex, and ambiguous.

As a rule of thumb at Institute for the Future, we look back at least 50 years every time we do a ten-year forecast. We look for patterns of change. We look for thresholds of change. We look for signals that precede the future. We look in particular for what seems ready to take off, even if it has failed many times before. We look for stories that connect to the signals and give clues about how this particular future could come to pass. As novelist William Gibson said so eloquently, "The future's already here. It's just unevenly distributed."

Here is a summary of the core disruptions I am forecasting over the next decade:

We are on a twisting path toward distributed everything

- **Increasing speed, frequency, scope, and scale of disruption**
- **Explosive connectivity—way beyond today's connectivity**
- **Asymmetric upheaval—few clear patters of disruption**

FIGURE 4 Anything that can be distributed will be distributed.

To understand the future, leaders need to listen for signals while filtering out noise. You can listen only for things you are able to hear, however. Leaders need to be tuned to listening for things that don't fit in interesting ways—even if they don't fit that leader's preconception of how they are or how they might be. Leaders must be sense makers in a world that will differ profoundly from what they have experienced before.

Much of the present is noise. And, to make it more complicated, the future that is already here often will take a long time to scale. The signals of the present need to be considered within the context of the past, the constraints of the present, and the opportunities of the future. On rare occasion, an author is able to make sense of the noise of the present and reveal the directions of change.

Kevin Kelly does just that in his book, *The Inevitable: Understanding 12 Technological Forces That Will Shape Our Future.* This amazing guide introduces the technologies that will challenge us over the next decade.

Increased *sharing* both encourages increased *flowing* and depends on it. *Cognifying* requires *tracking. Screening* is inseparable for *interacting.* The verbs themselves are *remixed,* and all of these actions are variations on the process of *becoming.* They are a unified field of motion.

These forces are trajectories, not destinies. They offer no predictions of where we end up. They tell us simply that in the near future we are headed inevitably in these directions. (Kelly 2016)

I am focused on the leadership literacies that will be necessary to thrive in this kind of world.

The connective media of today are just beginning to turn into the next waves of much more intense disruption. I think of today's internet as the world's largest market test for the futures that are about to happen. I am inspired by one enveloping disruption that will amplify everything else over the next decade: the future force toward distributed everything. (See Figure 4.)

CHAPTER 1

The *New Literacy* of Looking Backward from the Future

LEADERS WHO HAVE THE LITERACY OF LOOKING BACKWARD from the future can say

- I can see long-term patterns of change ten years ahead, beyond the noise of the present.
- I bring a futures perspective to every conversation.
- I believe that a futures perspective makes better decisions in the present more likely.
- I develop my clarity but moderate my certainty.

I grew up as a basketball player in Geneva—a very small town west of Chicago—in the basketball-crazy state of Illinois. I was a rebounder and was taught to "always look long" coming off the boards. "If the long pass is there, take it!" my coaches would say over and over in the spirit of the fast break. Since I was young, I've been taught to look long. When I finished my humble college basketball career at the University of Illinois, I started looking long beyond the basketball court, and it turned out I was better at it off the court than on.

I have been immersed in the future since 1968, when I was a student at the same divinity school that Martin Luther King Jr. attended, Crozer Theological Seminary—then in Chester, Pennsylvania. Ever since then, I have focused my life ten years ahead.

At Crozer, I was a research assistant for a conference on religion and the future organized by Professor Kenneth Cauthen, one of the first theologians to create open dialogues between religion and science. At that conference, I got to carry the bags (literally) for the world's leading futurists. I have a vivid memory of running out under the helicopter blades to get the suitcase of Herman Kahn, the founder of the Hudson Institute and the father of modern scenario planning. I was particularly moved by the title of his most famous books: *Thinking about the Unthinkable.* Looking backward from the future will help leaders think about the unthinkable and, increasingly, it will be important to do just that.

I remember going into Professor Cauthen's office and seeing a newsletter from the World Future Society announcing the formation of Institute for the Future in 1968. I remember thinking, that's where I want to work. Five years later, that's where I was working—and I still am working there.

In between Crozer and Institute for the Future, I had another futures immersion experience at Northwestern University in an interdisciplinary PhD program. When I arrived, I imagined myself becoming a sociology of religion professor, with a focus on religion and the future. My program required that I take all the basic courses of any sociology PhD student. My interests, however, stretched into the psychology, religion, and computer science departments; and at Northwestern, interdisciplinary work was encouraged.

While I was at Northwestern in the early 1970s, the predecessor to the internet, the ARPANET (Advanced Research Projects Agency Network), was just coming to life. I became completely enthralled by the implications of network connectivity for people, organizations, and the world. While my home sociology department at Northwestern still used computer punch cards, I was able to walk over to the computer center and interact directly—though crudely by today's standards—with one of the world's largest computers.

Jamais Cascio, my colleague at IFTF, likens futures research to getting a vaccination. You understand that there are dangers out there and you want to vaccinate yourself against them. To extend the analogy, looking long is like fitness training in addition to getting a vaccination. You should not only get the best vaccinations available, but you should also exercise to prepare your mind and your body for the future.

A ten-year futures perspective is built into our way of life at the institute. Looking long is using foresight to provoke insight and action.

Jeremy Kirshbaum, another IFTF colleague, likens futures research to earthquake forecasting. Earthquakes are inevitable but also unpredictable. We have lots of historical data behind them, but they are still unpredictable in their nature. However, we can identify zones where you shouldn't build your house out of brick. More importantly with earthquakes, there are readiness disciplines and resilience practices that we can use to prepare.

Figure 5 summarizes the new literacy of looking backward from the future. I first published the Foresight to Insight to Action Cycle in a Berrett-Koehler book called *Get There Early* (Johansen 2007), but it has evolved considerably since then.

In the first version of the cycle, I had arrows that went clockwise only. Over years of practicing, I've realized that this process can go either direction. Also, I decided that arrows were too symmetrical for the realities of foresight to insight to action. After you've had an insight, that insight might cause you to revise your forecast. After you've moved ahead with an action, your experience might cause you to revise your insight or your foresight. Making the future is filled with twists and turns.

Foresight, inevitably, links in some way to hindsight. Think of hindsight as our banks of prior knowledge. Hindsight includes experience, which can be both a source of insight and a burden. Hindsight can be a cognitive anchoring in the past, and it can be a stimulus for innovation. Hindsight can keep us from seeing futures we cannot imagine.

It is revealing to notice that the word *history* has the word *story* embedded in it. Futures research is, in a real sense, storytelling about the history of

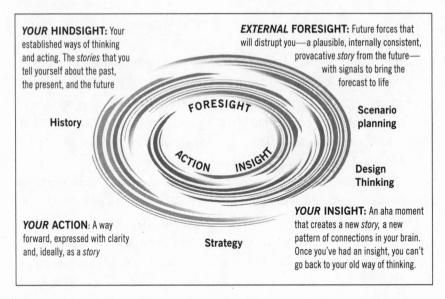

FIGURE 5 Nobody can predict the future.

the future—the present that hasn't happened yet. It was novelist Ursula K. Le Guin, an eloquent futures storyteller herself, who said, "Story is our only boat for sailing on the river of time" (Le Guin 1994).

Master storyteller Kendall Haven, one of the key players on a recent project to explore the neuroscience of storytelling, taught me that we all have our own personal neural story net that shapes our hindsight and our view of the world (Haven 2014). As we experience new things, we always run them up against our personal neural story net to see what fits and what does not. More open-minded people have flexible neural story nets that allow them to see alternative futures, while others are trapped in their old stories—no matter what new experiences they may have. Thinking systematically about the future helps us to loosen up, keep an open mind, and question our own assumptions.

But this is tough work. Leaders at innovative companies often try out new technologies too early, and their experiments fail. Years later, those same leaders are likely to remember their earlier failures when someone comes to them to propose use of a new technology. "We tried that years ago and it didn't work," they say—and they are correct. Yes, they tried it too early, but that doesn't mean that same innovation—or some variation—won't work later, when the timing is right.

Traditionally innovative companies often miss the biggest potential impacts of a new technology or innovation once it finally occurs. Innovation often involves timing. A failed technology in one period can become a giant success later on. Those early innovators often watch in frustration as later (often less innovative) companies get the benefit of a delayed innovation. Hindsight—even accurate hindsight—can limit foresight. It is dangerous to assume that what didn't work before doesn't work now. Often, what didn't work before does work now. Leaders need to keep their minds open.

Foresight is a plausible, internally consistent, provocative story from the future, with signals to bring it to life. Notice that *story* is recurring. Futurists tell stories of possibility about the future, as if they had some special access to it. Some foresight is quantitative, but even quantitative forecasts should be wrapped in good stories in order to reach wide audiences.

Foresight should provoke people, but with a tone of humility. One of the things I don't like about some futurists is that they seem to relish in making other people feel stupid. I believe that the best futurists provoke insights for others in a way that is both provocative and humble. The best futurists, like great leaders, both inspire and empower. The best foresight provokes insight for others. In my talks and workshops, I try to frighten people at the start but empower them by the end.

Having a sense of humor about the future is also important. Some futurists take themselves so seriously. The future is unpredictable, so it is imperative that we stay humble. Humility leads to a sense of humor, since future forecasts will often be wrong—or even right for the wrong reasons or right but in the wrong time frame. Often, the future happens in unexpected ways even if the overall direction of change is forecast accurately. Both humility and humor are important aspects of leadership, and a futures perspective presents opportunities for both. Studying the future can be fun.

When we do a custom forecast at Institute for the Future, we provide the independent outside-in foresight. We look at least ten years ahead at external future forces likely to disrupt a particular organization or topic. For example, we've done custom forecasts recently on external future forces likely to disrupt food security and another forecast focused on poverty. Our job is foresight, but insight is the responsibility of those who use our forecasts. We are not experts in their industries; we are not even experts in the present. We provide an outside-in perspective, but it is their job to listen for the future and allow themselves to be provoked.

Insight is an aha moment that creates a new pattern of connections in your brain. Creating insight is a lot harder than generating ideas. Ideas bubble out, but insight is rare. Ideas are wonderful, but they are easy compared to insight. Insight is often hard uncomfortable work. Consider Verlyn Flieger's insight about Tolkien, one of the world's great storytellers:

> *Turn*, let us not forget, is the word Tolkien uses for the moment of change in fairy-stories, the moment of becoming. It is reversal, metanoia, felt before the mind can grasp it, before the apprehension of the happy ending and the consolation. (Flieger 1933)

The goal of futures thinking is to use foresight to induce the kind of head-jerking turn that happens as you read a great story or play a great game: an abrupt shift in your thinking. Once you have had an insight, you can't go back to your old way of thinking. Insight changes you. Ultimately, foresight is about sense making in a future world where sense is in short supply.

The way to evaluate a futurist is to ask if the foresight provoked an insight that led to a better decision in the present. The way to evaluate a fortune teller is to ask whether or not the foresight actually happened. Futurists should not and cannot predict the future. Instead, futurists should provoke insight.

Right after 9/11, I was asked by Walt Disney World to do a forecast of the future of fun in theme parks, with a focus on Walt Disney World in Orlando.* Parents, especially right after 9/11, were very concerned about the safety of taking their kids into large crowds. The kids, however, just wanted to have fun.

Our foresight was that the fun would become increasingly important for everyone because of all the uncertainty in the world around us. The VUCA world, our forecast suggested, will make the shared experience of fun and

---

* I did this custom forecast with Dr. Mark Schar, now at Stanford University.

fear even more important. Everyone wants to have immersive fun experiences, but parents will be very concerned about safety.

The insight that came out of this custom forecast was that a theme park had to be a place where kids could be *safely scared*. Walt Disney World offers an experience that is extremely safe but still scary in a way that kids love. Certainly, Walt Disney World—particularly EPCOT—is able to turn this insight into action. We never know exactly how our foresight inspires insight and action—there are always many variables—but the link between foresight, insight, and action seems clear in this case.

IFTF did a custom forecast for Procter & Gamble in the early days of biotech. Our forecast was that biotech would disrupt P&G, especially the detergent and hair care businesses. I presented this custom forecast to the CEO and his global leadership council. Their insight at that meeting was that none of the top people had enough biotech background to make good business decisions about this emerging future that we forecast (and which has now happened).

The action that came out of that combination of foresight and insight was something they called the biotech reverse mentoring program: we paired the top twelve people at P&G with young P&G biotech scientists. Each pair met about once a month for a year. The leaders from the executive floor went out to the labs—often for the first time. The young scientists went to the executive floor—often for the first time. The scientists were never the same afterward—and neither were the executives. The scientists had a new appreciation of the decisions that the executives faced—and this was a particularly difficult period for P&G. The executives understood the basic science at a deep-enough level to understand the forecast regarding the impact of biotech on their businesses. A. G. Lafley, one of those executives, went on to become one of the most successful CEOs in P&G history, and his mentor became one of P&G's leaders in sustainability. The biotech perspective that began with this mentoring program was spread through a community of practice and is now embedded in P&G's strategy. Foresight had provoked insight that led to action—with very good business results.

The purpose of ten-year futures thinking is to come up with a way forward, expressed with clarity and ideally as a story. The best way to lead in a disruptive world is to be very clear where you're going, tell a great story about it, and then be very flexible about how you bring that future to life. In the military, this way of thinking and acting is called *commander's intent* or *mission command*, but I like the term *clarity* a lot better for business or other non-military organizations.

Collective moments of insight—when people come to the same realization together at the same time—are often the most powerful. Foresight is a wonderful way to provoke insight even if you don't agree with the forecast. You can argue with any forecast, but it is best to resist the temptation. Some of the best forecasts will be those you don't like. The most useful approach is to assume that foresight is plausible, internally consistent, and provocative. What are your insights, given these external future forces? Repeat the process with an alternative forecast if you are not satisfied with the first.

The reason you look long is to develop the perspective necessary to come up with a good plan of action, a way forward, expressed with clarity and ideally as a story. The big lesson is to be very clear where you're going, but very flexible how you get there. Action should animate you. That's the basic discipline of looking backward from the future—but still acting now.

Trends consultancies and the business press tend to start from today's world and work a few years out. Some of these consultancies focus on fashion or fads, which are short-term shifts in preferences or behavior. In contrast, I'm suggesting that leaders leap ahead and focus ten or more years ahead, then work backward to identify opportunities today—given the external future forces of the next decade. Anyone can do this, not just professional futurists. In most fields, there is so much noise in the present that it is very hard to get a clear view of what's going on or where things are going.

At IFTF, we call this process *Forecaster's Haiku*. A haiku is an artfully concise Japanese poem of three lines and seventeen syllables (five, seven, five). It involves considerable art to create headline summaries for each forecast that are provocative without turning people off. The headlines also need to be familiar enough to be understood without sounding like the same old thing. While our foresight is focused ten years out, the insights and actions that result will be designed to inform current decision making.

For some forecasts, we literally use haiku as a discipline for pulling out the essence of a forecast. For example, we did a 30-year forecast on the future of food security recently. One of the big themes was what we called the *programmable world*, where digital innovation comes to the world of food science. Here is the haiku we created:

Unlock potential

When physical is programmed

Like digital world

Figure 6 is a summary of the shift toward looking backward from the future.

Current Literacy	Future Literacy
• Leaders focus on the present first, then think out gradually as far as they can toward the future.	• The best leaders will jump ten or more years ahead and then work backward from the future.
• How can I look ten years ahead when I can't even make sense of the present?	• Long-term forecasting is easier than short-term—leaders wil have to look long to make sense of the VUCA world.
• Leaders who express certainty are viewed as strong leaders.	• Certainty will be suspect, but the best leaders will have clarity.

FIGURE 6 The new literacy of looking backward from the future, to act now with clarity—but not certainty

Looking backward from the future will require many skills. In *Leaders Make the Future*, I identified ten future leadership skills that I believe will be required for leaders to thrive in the future. Two of these skills—clarity and dilemma flipping—will be particularly important for looking backward from the future.

Looking backward from the future will help you find your *clarity*.

Clarity: Ability to see through messes and contradictions to a future that others cannot yet see.

On the weekend of Martin Luther King Jr.'s birthday in 2015, I saw the movie *Selma*, and I read the book by Tavis Smiley about the last year of Dr. King's life. Smiley studied the Civil Rights Movement and concluded that during that year, Dr. King was rejected by most of the people who were close to him (Ritz & Smiley 2010). Thinking of all the wonderful things Dr. King did, it made me sad to think those closest to him decided that he was going off track. They thought he was getting interested in too many different causes—the march against poverty, opposition to the Vietnam War, and environmental issues. He lost his clarity, they said. Rather, Dr. King had a *different* clarity that some of his closest colleagues had missed.

Dr. King pushed back and reminded his followers that achieving civil rights was *part* of his higher calling—his long view included a deep commitment to social justice. Racism, poverty, and militarism were *all* social justice issues.

Here is a corporate example of clarity and the need for a long view: A. G. Lafley, the former CEO of Procter & Gamble, was a master in clarity. He was very good at using foresight to provoke his own insight and action, stating his clarity, and being flexible in how he executed that clarity.

When he first came in as CEO Lafley revived an old P&G motto: "The consumer is boss." He repeated this phrase many times per day, always with great enthusiasm. Clarity of expression requires the enthusiasm of a Broadway actor performing the same play again and again but always with inspired emotion. Many leaders tire of telling the same story again and again, but repetition is very important to spreading the message of clarity.

At that time P&G was facing big challenges, and their internal R&D was under-delivering. Lafley said that half of the new ideas should come from the outside. He told people that he would measure them, that he would publicly announce when P&G achieved a goal, and that whoever did it would publish an article in the *Harvard Business Review* about how it was done. He delivered a clear, radical statement of direction and then allowed a lot of flexibility about how to do it. The very successful program that came to be called "Connect and Develop" was the result, but that came out only as people raced ahead in pursuit of the clarity that Lafley both embodied and expressed constantly—always with contagious enthusiasm (Huston & Sakab 2006).

Clarity has always been important for leaders, but it's never been so difficult as it will be over the next decade. Being clear in an extremely disruptive world will be much harder than it was in simpler times.

Looking backward from the future will increase your ability to do the kind of dilemma flipping that will become increasingly necessary in the VUCA world.

Dilemma Flipping: Ability to turn dilemmas—which, unlike problems, cannot be solved—into advantages and opportunities.

The next decade will be loaded with dilemmas, and leaders will need to figure out how to flip them into opportunities.

To do dilemma flipping, you have got to like the space between judging too soon and deciding too late. If you're not sure if it's a problem or a dilemma when you're facing a challenge, it is better to assume it's a dilemma. If it turns out it's a problem you can solve, that's great. But if you think it's a problem and it turns out to be a dilemma, you're in trouble, because you have set expectations as if you're going to solve it, but you won't be able to.

Chris Folayan started a company to sell items from international retailers to Africans across the continent.* The idea sounds so simple, but it was really innovative. Folayan looked long to see that Africans had more spending power and wanted more global consumer goods. The dilemma here was that global companies feared the risk of entering a historically unpredictable marketplace that was unfamiliar with ecommerce. MallforAfrica has found out how to turn that to its advantage and has been very successful. It is now expanding the relationship with retailers to sell African items in the United States. Whether or not Folayan has long-term commercial success, MallforAfrica is a signal of a new kind of retailing on a global scale.

Looking long makes it clear that global digital infrastructure will be wildly varied for the foreseeable future. The sources of innovation won't be just Silicon Valley and other high-tech zones. Rather, innovation will come from Africa and other regions of the world that are dealing with constraints that force that innovation. For example, the power bank phone is common in West Africa. It handles up to three SIM cards, is 3G enabled, and has an

* www.mallforafrica.com

enormous battery pack that can last for weeks when the power grid is faulty, which is a frequent occurrence there. This basic-level phone is available for around twenty USD and appears under several brand names. It is unclear who originally created it, but whoever did so was looking long and stimulated by a challenging dilemma that got flipped creatively.

A final dilemma example is health care in the United States, which is not a problem that can be solved. The health care system can be *improved*, but it can't be solved, so problem-solving language is inappropriate. When facing a complex challenge like health care, it is very important to be really careful about language. If the challenge you are facing is a dilemma, or even if you think it *might* be, you should call it a *dilemma* and use dilemma language. The VUCA world will be loaded with dilemmas, which leaders will have to deal with. There will still be many problems that can be solved, but they will be solved mostly by people who work for leaders, in some sense of the term "work for." Leaders will deal mostly with dilemmas.

CHAPTER 2

Moving Toward a Future That Rewards Clarity— But Punishes Certainty

LOOKING BACKWARD FROM THE FUTURE WILL SEEM unnatural for many leaders today—they are so present focused—but the tools for thinking about the future systematically are improving rapidly, and the need for looking backward from the future is growing. Young people— especially those who have grown up as gamers—will have a competitive advantage in this future. It will become possible to look even further into the future, to see deeper patterns and directions of change, and to avoid simplistic thinking.

SURPRISE Ten-year forecasting is easier than one-year forecasting.

People often ask me: "How can you do ten-year forecasting? I can't even forecast one year ahead!" Surprisingly, it is actually easier to look long than to look close in. There is too much noise in the present.

The more complex the future, the further ahead leaders will need to look. Given the external future forces of the next decade, leaders will need to expand their leadership literacy by looking *really* long. Fortunately, the next generation of leaders will be gamefully prepared for this to happen.

Leaders will face an increasingly uncertain future, even while many of those they lead will crave certainty. Looking long and working backward from the future can help sift out the shards of certainty from which leaders can create clarity. This chapter considers what will happen in the years ahead when we look backward from the future.

Let's begin with an example of a ten-year forecast that is almost certain to happen: In ten years sensors will be everywhere, sensors will be very cheap, many sensors will be connected, and some sensors will be in our bodies. Most importantly, we will also have improved ability to make sense out of all this new sensor data.

Ubiquitous sensors will disrupt how leaders lead. The world of sensors is going to give us an incredible amount of data and the tools to make sense of all that data. If the sensors are accurate, they will create really interesting opportunities and really interesting challenges. If the sensors aren't accurate and people trust the misinformation that is generated, that will create different challenges. Corporations will have to respond to misinformation, but people may be skeptical about their responses. The new world of sensors will be both more revealing and more confusing. Sensors will both enhance and corrode trust—depending on how they are used.

Over a ten-year period, this forecast about sensors is difficult to refute—even though it is uncertain just what will happen with sensors in the next year or two, let alone who will make money from whatever happens. We need to look into the future with an open mind, but the challenge for leaders is to come back from that forecast future with insight and a plan of action in the present.

In the case of this forecast, there is clarity about where sensors are going but uncertainty about how we will get there and what it will mean once we have ubiquitous sensors. If you want to know about the future of sensors, don't go to the Consumer Electronics Show—the giant Las Vegas extravaganza held each January—because you will be overwhelmed by the present, and there is just too much noise in the present.

By looking backward from the future, leaders will be forced to come to terms with the existence of other futures and recognize that people will live

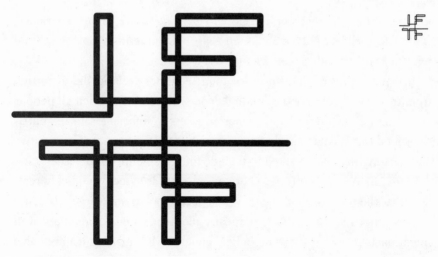

FIGURE 7 For most people, Institute for the Future's logo becomes clearer the farther they hold it away—just like thinking about the future. The smaller version in the upper right is much easier to read than the larger one.

differently then. Certainly, some things will not change, even in the most uncertain of times. But leaders will need to distinguish between what will change and what will not, between what *should* change and what should not.

Jean Hagan designed Institute for the Future's logo on an Etch-a-Sketch. If you look at it up close, it is hard to read. For most people, the logo becomes clearer the farther they hold it away—just like thinking about the future. The logo in the upper right of Figure 7 is much easier to read than the larger logo, even though it is much smaller. This logo embodies the brand story of Institute for the Future.

How Far Ahead Should You Look?

For every custom forecast that we do at Institute for the Future, a key question is always how far ahead the forecast should look. We want the forecast to be beyond the planning horizon for current strategy but still close enough in to be believable. In almost fifty years of forecasting, IFTF has found that ten years is usually the sweet spot. However, ten years is just too far for some of our clients, so we forecast five years (or five to ten years) into the future. But that feels too close to me. The future, in my experience, starts to come clear only at about ten years out. Sometimes looking beyond ten years will provide a view that is even clearer.

In our forecast on the future of food security, we used the definition from the 1996 World Food Summit: "Food security exists when all people, at all times, have physical and economic access to sufficient, safe and nutritious food that meets their dietary needs and food preferences for an active and healthy life."* We wanted to include food availability, food access, and food use. In Western Europe, where our client was based, we quickly realized that the topic of food security was deeply polarizing, largely because of perceptions about GMO (genetically modified) foods. Some very well intentioned people had strong beliefs about GMO, making it impossible to even have a conversation about food chemistry. Without a conversation about food chemistry, it was very difficult to do a forecast about food security and global hunger.

Our resolution on the topic of food security was to look 30 years ahead, instead of only 10, which made the conversation less polarized. Even those who view GMO as a yes/no choice in the upcoming decade could see the value of including a discussion of food chemistry if we looked 30 years ahead. If you look 30 years ahead, you will see that GMO is not a yes/no choice but a spectrum of food chemistry choices. Certainly, there will be good GMO and bad GMO, but that is not apparent today—particularly for those convinced either of its evil or its promise.

Sometimes, focusing on the future can help people move beyond the polarities of the present. The best forecasts will begin with a conversation involving foresight to insight to action, so it is very important to go far enough out to begin a great conversation and not get stuck in the polarities of the present. Fortunately, the next generation of young people seems likely—even beyond the normal open-mindedness of youth—to find it much easier to look long.

The 2010 Threshold

Around 2010, the transformation from separate digital tools to media ecology accelerated. Separate tools began to flow together into new media envi-

---

* http://www.fao.org/forestry/13128-0e6f36f27e0091055bec28ebe830f46b3.pdf.

ronments. The threshold for new media disruption was crossed early in the new century, when new patterns of disruption began to emerge and new generations of young people came of age. Digital and connective *technologies* and *tools* began the long process of turning into *media*. The nature of the innovation ecology shifted during this transition period.

Young people who experienced this shift at a seminal time of their lives— particularly kids on the verge of becoming adults—will play an elevated role in what happens over the next decade, looking out to 2027.

Being a leader with people who have experienced this shift will be different in important ways, even though nobody yet knows just how different. As these young people become leaders, they will have capabilities that will be beyond those of us who are digital immigrants—even people like me who grew up with the early internet.

To be clear, I'm not arguing that it was an abrupt snap from off to on. The transformation became apparent to me only in retrospect, looking back. It is debatable just when the threshold was crossed, but it was approximately in 2010. The younger you are, however, the stronger the effect and the more prepared you will be to look really long.

Around 2010, the tools of connectivity began to blend together to seed a new media ecology of connectivity. When the iPhone was introduced in 2007, Apple wasn't just offering a telephone; it was introducing a digital appliance with a dizzying array of uses, including one still used by older people like me—to make a phone call.

Another early signal event in this transformation was Apple's App Store, created in 2008. Then, around 2010, the connective tools started mixing together and transforming into connective media ecology.

We had early digital tools for connectivity back then, with a wide range of failed attempts preceding them. All of these technologies linked in some way to packet switching and the upcoming age of the internet.

The threshold period around 2010 was characterized by

- early-stage—still very crude—social technologies
- provocative but limited interfaces through early tablets and smart phones
- early stage blended-reality abilities to overlay in-person experiences with digital filters

- vivid video gaming interfaces that were already far more advanced than typical office systems of the day

These early media provided a hint of what it would be like to have a supercomputer on your shoulder—or in your glasses or contact lenses—as you experience life.

Questions started to emerge: What if we really did have a virtual overlay over the physical world? What if we could bring a world of computing power to the virtual overlay to help us make choices and filter everyday life? What if computing was truly mobile? What if anything could be a screen? What if we had intelligent agents that guided us through life, according to criteria that we established?

Whatever media ecology you have around you when you come of age will shape the rest of your life. I would argue that most kids become adults between age 13 and 15, depending on the kid and depending on the culture. The younger you are and the richer the media ecology around you, the stronger the impact will be on you.

I believe that young people who became adults in 2010 or later will grow up with different ways of thinking, ways of learning, ways of interacting, and ways of living. They will have powerful capabilities to look long and not be stuck in the futures that adults are imagining.

I'm really optimistic about those people who are 21 and younger in 2017. In fact, the younger they are, the more optimistic I am. Those who were born in 1996 or later will be most prepared for the future. This is not a sharp generational line. Rather, it is a fuzzy threshold where isolated technologies transformed into a new media ecology that is becoming a new context for living. The new media threshold of 2010 was clear only in retrospect. It was both gradual and dramatic. The new media ecology that emerged is now the context for thinking about and planning for the future. I believe that the kids who became adults in 2010 or later will make a better future.

The directional shift for this future is clearly from less digital to more digital to *so* digital that the word *digital* will become unnecessary. In fact, over the next decade, the word itself will disappear, since virtually everything will have a digital element. The big transformation will be from digital tools to connective media that will be so pervasive that people will wear them like jewelry. Digital media will so ubiquitous that they are invisible.

I wrote a book called *Groupware* in 1988. Nobody talks about groupware anymore because it's just what our computers do. As group functionality got built into everyday computing systems and became basic to how we work and live, the word *groupware* became unnecessary. The word *digital* will follow a similar path, not to extinction but to being so pervasive that it is assumed.

Already, it is too late to have a digital strategy per se. Organizations will need strategies that have digital capabilities built in.

Clarity vs. Certainty

In a highly uncertain world, it will be very easy for leaders to confuse clarity with certainty. Many people—including many leaders—just aren't prepared for the speed and scale of disruption they will be facing over the next decade. In this future world, *simple* will be good, but *simplistic* will be dangerous.

Simplistic solutions will become more alluring as the degree of uncertainty rises. An urgent need for what psychologists call *cognitive closure* can lure anyone into simplistic logic that confuses clarity and certainty.* Everything in the VUCA world will be risky, but clarity will offer lower risk, whereas certainty will create higher risk.

What is the difference between clarity and certainty? Clarity is usually expressed in stories, while certainty is usually expressed in rules. Rigid rules can get leaders in a lot of trouble in the VUCA world, while stories encourage people to engage. Clarity is lucid and coherent; certainty is definite and brittle. Great stories invite people to add color within the boundaries of the story. Rules punish people who violate them. Stories sing. Rules shout.

---

* "This term was coined by the social psychologist Arie Kruglanski, who eventually defined it as 'individuals' desire for a firm answer to a question and an aversion toward ambiguity,' a drive for certainty in the face of a less than certain world. When faced with heightened ambiguity and a lack of clear-cut answers, we need to know—and as quickly as possible." From Maria Konnikova, *The New Yorker* (April 30, 2013) in an article exploring why we need answers in the face of terrorist events. See also *The Psychology of Close Mindedness*, Arie Kruglanski, New York: Psychology Press, 2004.

Neuroscience has a big cautionary lesson for know-it-all leaders: beware when you are certain about anything. Neuroscientists have a term for certainty: *knowing we know*. If you ever know you know something, be careful. If a leader speaks with absolute certainty about anything but core value commitments, beware. If you encounter a person who uses the word "absolutely" a lot, beware.

Neuroscientist Robert Burton's *On Being Certain: Believing You Are Right Even When You Are Not*, explores why people in controlled laboratory experiments continue to believe they are right, even if it is demonstrated to them that they are actually wrong. He has put people in experimental settings using fMRI (functional magnetic resonance imaging) where they can see they are wrong, but their brains keep telling them that they are right. Dr. Burton explains this counter-intuitive phenomenon in this way:

> *Despite how certainty feels*, it is neither a conscious choice nor even a thought process. Certainty and similar states of "knowing we know" arise out of involuntary brain mechanisms that, like love or anger, function independently of reason. (Burton 2010)

What this means for leaders is that if you *feel* certain you are reaching a rational conclusion, your feelings may not be accurately reflecting the reality of the situation at all. What looks and feels to you for all the world like a sure thing may be anything but.

I had a very disturbing personal experience of this phenomenon. When I was the president of Institute for the Future, the hiring decision that I made that I was most certain about, the one that I had complete confidence in, was the worst hiring decision I ever made. I knew that I knew so strongly that I didn't listen to the people close to me who questioned me.

What do you do as a leader to hedge against such a mistake? There is something really obvious you can do: give a trusted person who is close to you permission to question and challenge you. You need somebody whose opinion you value to be able to tell you you're wrong.

As I was finishing writing this book, a *New Yorker* article by Elizabeth Kolbert came out summarizing three new books that reach conclusions similar to those of Robert Burton. But these books come from the perspective of the cognitive sciences rather than neuroscience. Called "Why Facts

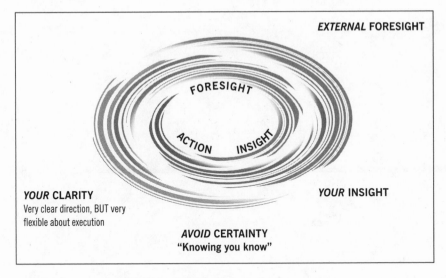

EXTERNAL FORESIGHT

FORESIGHT

ACTION INSIGHT

YOUR CLARITY
Very clear direction, BUT very
flexible about execution

YOUR INSIGHT

AVOID CERTAINTY
"Knowing you know"

FIGURE 8 A summary of looking backward from the future

Don't Change Our Minds," this article starts from the common concept of *confirmation bias* (it is easier to believe things that are consistent with our previously held beliefs), which is now being reframed as "myside bias." New research shows that "people believe that they know way more than they actually do. What allows us to persist in this belief is other people" (Kolbert 2017).

Knowing you know will be very dangerous. Leaders will have to develop their clarity but moderate their certainty. This will be very difficult in a highly disruptive world where people long for certainty. Seek out clarity in leaders, but beware of certainty.

Looking backward from the future will become much more important for leaders. The next generation of leaders is likely to find looking long easier than older leaders. Young people who became adults in 2010 or later are likely to have a competitive advantage over the rest of us.

CHAPTER 3

The *New Literacy* of Voluntary Fear Engagement

LEADERS WHO HAVE THE LITERACY OF VOLUNTARY FEAR can say

- I am comfortable with and adept at gaming, simulation, improvisation, and role-playing.
- I am committed to immersive learning to engage with communities where I lead.
- I practice my leadership skills in low-risk settings.

Gaming, grit, and guilds are three very old concepts that will be re-imagined over the next decade to help leaders prepare for the VUCA world.

Jane McGonigal defines games as "obstacles that we volunteer to overcome" (McGonigal 2011). Gameful engagement with the future can safely immerse you in a world of fear, so you can practice ways to lead. The best response to fear is to engage with it directly, rather than avoid it. Games can give leaders a way to do just that, in realistic but low-risk ways. Good

games—like good stories—are characterized by emotionally laden attention. A good game is also a good story, but as a player you get to be *in* the
story—not just read the story.

A gamer's mantra that I hear often from leadership development experience designers: when people are laughing, they are learning. Experienced
game designers recognize a certain kind of laugh and a certain kind of smile
that seems to accompany deep learning. In other circles this state of engaged
learning is referred to as a state of *flow*. Activities that are risky, hard to
accomplish, and stimulate a sense of discovery often have a natural flow to
them (Csíkszentmihályi 1996).

Guilds allow people to play and learn together. They are all about connection, but it is connection in the context of the game and the skills that
are necessary to succeed in the game. Guilds go way back in time, when
they were associations of craftsmen, tradesmen, or merchants, often with
considerable power in their communities. Guild members have always had
a shared purpose and a nurtured kinship for mutual benefit. Like the guilds
of old, modern guilds allow craftspeople to share their craft and learn from
each other. Scott Andrews, a former guild leader for the popular video game
World of Warcraft, describes guilds this way:

> Guilds bind players together into a social network and enable those play-
> ers to work in concert for a common purpose: to tackle the incredible
> group-oriented content designed by game developers. (Andrews 2010)

Video gaming communities, particularly those involved in the massive
multiplayer online role-playing games (MMORPGs), have adopted the
concept of a guild and many of its ancient practices. In a game like *World
of Warcraft*, almost everyone you encounter is a member of a guild, from
characters who are just starting out to those elite players who are battling
the world's greatest evil.

Guilds are a lot like what, earlier in my career, were called *communities of
practice* (Lave & Wenger 1991). The term is still used in some corporations
where I work, but seems to have declined in popularity. The term *guilds*, a
much older term, may replace communities of practice. What's important is
the practice, not what it comes to be called.

At Electronic Arts, there are guilds for analytics, for producers, for development directors, and for quality assurance. Members of guilds learn from each other's successes and mistakes. Guilds work across studios.

Guilds are about learning, community, and power. They are not necessarily focused on winning the game, or being the best, or being the largest. Some might aspire to those things, but the fundamental purpose of a guild is to make a network that enables players to have a positive experience through social connections. Similarly, in the real world of the future, guilds—or whatever they come to be called—will allow people to learn from each other and learn together.

Playing Through Fear Positively

If you don't have some fear about the future, you're not paying attention. Fear is not a bad thing. It's what you *do* with your fear that can turn bad. Leaders must learn to play through their fear and develop effective and efficient responses, turning fear into something positive. Leaders will need guilds because the world is becoming an increasingly scary place. Being a good guild member in the real world will require leaders to go through voluntary fear exposure in order to be a stronger link in the chain. Guilds build grit. Players can be safely scared in the interest of developing their own readiness and resilience. Games can be safe zones for learning. By *safe zones*, I don't mean places where leaders will be free from what upsets them. Rather, I mean a place where leaders can confront their fears and learn to play through them in a low-risk setting.

In a world of disruptive opportunity, leaders will need to learn how to practice voluntary fear exposure. They will need safe zones to practice their leadership skills and develop their capacities, knowledge, discipline, practices, perspective, and worldview.

The most advanced immersive learning experience in fear engagement that I've ever seen is at the National Training Center for the U.S. Army at Fort Irwin in the Mojave Desert. It's only a three-hour drive from Las Vegas, but it feels worlds away. Fort Irwin is a soldier's last stop before going to war. About the size of Rhode Island, it could be thought of as the world's largest video gaming parlor.

I got to visit and observe a war game that lasted for two weeks, twenty-four hours a day, with real tanks, real helicopters, and Afghan actors. The game itself was designed to be harder than real warfare so that when soldiers get into an actual combat situation, it should be easier for them than what they experienced at Fort Irwin.

In the war game that I observed at the Army's National Training Center, soldiers could actually come back to life after they were killed. I got to go out on the battlefield and interview the virtually dead. After Action Reviews (AARs) were conducted on the battlefield, allowing them to figure out how to do better the next time. AARs are built into the experience at Fort Irwin. The core questions are these: What was supposed to happen? What actually happened? Why was there a difference? What can we learn from this? (Darling et al. 2005) It surprised me that the military seems able to separate After Action Reviews from performance reviews. I have not seen a single company that is able to make that very important separation across the whole company and, unless you do, it is very hard to learn from your mistakes. I hope that at least a few companies have achieved this separation, at least in pockets of their organizations, but it has proven much more difficult in the corporate world than in the military.

The value of an AAR is not so much in the data that comes out of it; it's in the discipline that is created from systematically learning from experience. When the army first conducted AARs, it created this giant database that was supposed to collect all the lessons learned from After Action Reviews. I have talked to people who tried to use the data, and they admitted that the data itself was not very useful. What *was* extremely useful was the discipline that is taught from these emotionally engaging and physically challenging experiences.

At Fort Irwin, there is a home team that almost always wins called the Red Team. The Red Team is the enemy you never want to have to face, but you are able to learn from them and from your own mistakes, all with the faith that your mistakes won't be fatal. It is basically viewing a challenge from the adversary's point of view. By allowing teams within an organization the gameful space to act as a devil's advocate, organizations can simulate failure in cheap and quick ways. Much like a game, organizations can use that learning to improve their processes and eventual future outcomes. Red teaming like that practiced at Fort Irwin is now becoming a way to exercise and challenge existing strategies in many different settings (Zenko 2015).

The big insight here is that safe zones allow leaders a chance to practice very difficult circumstances with little risk. The combination of a vividly realistic safe zone, voluntary fear exposure by leaders, and red teaming that challenges you at every stage creates powerful learning.

We need that kind of experiential education in the business, government, and nonprofit worlds too. As best I can tell, business is way behind in the application of gameful engagement as a way of learning how to combat everyday fear, channel it in positive directions, and recover more quickly after stressful experiences.

A recurring theme in the military literature is how fear is best managed in the chaos of warfare:

> I hold it to be one of the simplest truths of war that the thing which enables an infantry soldier to keep going with his weapons is the near presence or the presumed presence of a comrade. The warmth which derives from human companionship is as essential to his employment of the arms with which he fights as is the finger with which he pulls a trigger or the eye with which he aligns his sights. The other man may be almost beyond hailing or seeing distance, but he must be there somewhere within a man's consciousness or the onset of demoralization is almost immediate. (Marshall 2000)

Often when I talk about the military's experience with gaming to top executives, they ask me for examples in the business world of organizations doing something similar. I think back on a visit I had to Facebook's campus with a group of top executives. As we walked the main promenade (which is reminiscent of Downtown Disney), they told us about Facebook Hackathons. Facebook employees are arranged into cross-disciplinary teams of people who would otherwise never work together. They are given a day to prototype and create a new Facebook feature. A process that normally takes a few months is condensed into a day to expose people to real stress and fear, but in a safe zone. One result that they shared with me was the ideation, prototyping, and fast-tracking of the Facebook Profile Picture filter that has been used as everything from celebration of athletic pride to a sign of global solidarity.

Voluntary Fear Engagement

Margee Kerr is one of the leading researchers now studying fear and its effects. In her book, she talks about some of the fear-invoking things she has experienced to challenge herself. For example, she walked out on a ledge 117 stories up on the CN Tower in Toronto, attached herself with a rope, and rappelled around the building doing exercises with a guide (Kerr 2015). Curiously, this experience has now been commercialized as the CN Tower Edge Walk, currently priced at $195 Canadian.* I'm afraid of heights and I cannot imagine doing this. Margee Kerr, however, studies fear; and in order to study fear, she seeks out safe zones where she can experience fear in a low-risk way. One big lesson is that voluntary fear exposure helps build resistance. I'm convinced, but not convinced enough to do the CN Tower Edge Walk.

Gaming, simulation, role-playing, improvisational theater, immersive travel, and similar experiences can help leaders create safe zones to practice their own leadership. Fear can keep people from doing what they need to do. Fear can prevent you from acting—even when you have to act. You can game your way through your fear. Your fear isn't likely to disappear, but you can learn how to manage it and still make the decisions you need to make. The challenge for leaders is to figure out how to practice leading in frightening future worlds in a low-risk way.

I had an experience with a group of executives recently where we created a voluntary fear exposure experience in virtual reality. Each participant, while immersed in a virtual reality (VR) headset, was lifted up the side of a tall building and asked to step off. One executive, however, jumped instead of stepping off. He broke a bone, and he could have killed himself if he had hit his head on the nearby table. My lesson: have spotters in VR experiences to ensure that the intersection between the physical and virtual world is indeed safe.

Jane McGonigal from IFTF is known as one of the world's leading game designers, and she is focused on the future. She introduced me to the term *gameful engagement*, which I like because it implies the use of fun and playful-

---

* "You! Pushing your personal limits to the Edge!" http://www.edgewalkcntower.ca.

ness to create an immersive learning opportunity. Gameful engagement can be in a digital video-gaming environment or in real life.

In today's business world, there is a buzz about *gamification*, a term that has come to mean adding an element of gaming to something you're already doing—or perhaps something people don't really want to do but get tricked into by a game-like interface. Gameful engagement should help people enjoy more what they want to do and learn.

I believe that gaming will become the most powerful learning medium in history. Again, the military already knows this. The fire services know this. The police services know this. Most corporations do not know this yet, except the airlines that use sophisticated simulators for pilot trainers, medical schools who use simulation to train surgeons, and a handful of others.

A gameful mindset, according to Jane McGonigal's latest research for her book *SuperBetter*, is associated with positives like these (McGonigal 2015):

- less depression and anxiety
- improved ability to cope with stress
- faster and fuller recovery from illness or injury
- closer relationships
- higher goal achievement
- new pattern development in the brain after trauma

Asked about the benefits of gaming, most parents of video gamers would be unlikely to generate this list. Certainly, in my opinion, many of today's video games are too sexual and too violent. But try to look beyond the content to the medium of gameful engagement. Also, consider the possibility that, if you have a very negative attitude toward video gaming, you might be playing the wrong games.

I recommend reading *SuperBetter* to get a sense of the spectrum of socially constructive games. Until I got to know Jane and her work, I didn't realize how many positive games are out there—and the number is growing. I'm hoping that the next wave of games will include ones that help leaders practice their leadership skills.

Games aren't new. People have always played games. What's new is the quality of digital interfaces. The interfaces are brilliant now, and they're so far ahead of anything we have in offices. Games will be characterized by emotionally laden attention, expressed in spectacular interfaces.

For some senior leaders, the word *game* just may not sound businesslike. ("We are a serious company—we don't play games!") When I encounter resistance to the word *gaming*, I generally go for a less controversial term like *immersive experience*, or *scenario*, or *simulation*. Basically, gaming is immersive engagement. Gaming is emotionally laden attention. Gaming is a good story, where the players get to be in the story. The language issues will be temporary.

Gaming—or whatever it comes to be called—will provide a rich pedagogy for learning, as has already been demonstrated convincingly in war gaming, emergency response simulations, pilot training, and surgical training.

The whole point of gameful engagement is to immerse yourself in a realistic but mock fearful environment and learn how to thrive, or at least push through it. Gameful engagement can be great learning, if you're playing the right games.

Gaming something means trying it out in a low-risk environment before doing it for real. You have to do that in a spirit that allows you to fail early, fail often, and fail cheaply.

Figure 9 is a summary of the shift toward voluntary fear exposure through gameful engagement:

The new leadership literacy of voluntary fear will require two leadership skills in particular: immersive learning ability and rapid prototyping.

Voluntary fear exposure will require leaders to develop and exercise their own immersive learning ability.

Immersive Learning Ability: The ability to immerse yourself in unfamiliar environments, to learn from them in a first-person way.

Lat Ware was diagnosed with attention deficit hyperactivity disorder (ADHD) at the age of five. For many years, he took a wide variety of drugs to control his symptoms, but they had some awful side effects, including suicidal urges. Games became a safe zone for Ware. He was not only able to immerse himself in games but also began designing his own. Now, he has come up with a game called *Throwing Trucks with Your Mind*, which has

Current Literacy	Future Literacy
• Serious companies and successful leaders don't play games.	• Leaders will need safe spaces to practice, in low-risk ways.
• Gaming is what we tell our kids not to do.	• The best leaders will be gritty gamers and prototypers.
• The millennials are the big disruption.	• Those people 21 or younger in 2017 will be the big disruptors.
• Don't even use the word *games*.	• Gaming will be the most powerful learning medium in history.

FIGURE 9 The new literacy of voluntary fear engagement

relieved his ADHD symptoms by making new connections in his brain. As I finish this book, the measurable impacts of playing the game, both on symptoms and patterns of thinking related to ADHD, are still unclear—but things look promising. By immersing himself in a gameful safe zone, Lat Ware created a new game that not only helps him but also helps others to learn.

This is an example of what education researcher Milton Chen calls "ed-*you*-cation." Dr. Chen has found that the most powerful form of learning begins from personal experience and personal interests (Chen 2010). Lat Ware had a very personal challenge that drew him into gaming. He created a game to improve his own situation, but the game he created now benefits many others.

Voluntary fear exposure will allow leaders to create low-risk spaces where they can practice rapid prototyping for innovation.

Rapid Prototyping: Creating quick early versions of innovations, with the expectation that later success will require early failures.

Rapid prototyping fits right into the Silicon Valley mantra to fail early, fail often, and fail cheaply. I have had the chance to work with IDEO a number of times over the years, and I've always been impressed with how early they begin prototyping. On a six-month product design project, they are likely to build the first prototype on the first afternoon and do hundreds of prototypes before they start to firm up the design.

This isn't always easy. I worked on a healthy foods project with them a decade ago, and it was difficult to actually prototype what a health food would look and taste like. They did many home visits and asked people to describe for them how they eat and how they make choices about what to eat. The IDEO team took detailed notes and created graphic displays with photos. By understanding how people make food choices, they were able to begin the prototyping process around user needs and wants. They focused on behaviors in the home, rather than relying on what people said. They also collected examples of existing products that were moving in the same direction they were pursuing. Current products can be viewed as prototypes for future products.

Rapid prototyping is blossoming in China, and many of these efforts are within gameful safe zones that allow people to explore new products, services, and experiences. For example, more than 200 livestreaming platforms are delivering tens of thousands of personal channels to the phone screens of tens of millions of young viewers. Hosts facilitate chats, meals, singing or dancing for their followers, deejaying, and all manner of personal performances. The hosts are paid in digital gifts (virtual cars, candy, and more), and profits are shared between platform and host, with some hosts earning thousands or tens of thousands of US dollars per month. These young people are rapidly prototyping ways to present their interests and identities in ways that also make money for them.

Think of this as one of the world's largest real-time youth experiments, testing out what kinds of activities can be live streamed and how much value can be personally generated from those streams. There will be many new forms of product placement, promotion, and advertising. This is an example of both gameful engagement in a safe zone and rapid prototyping of new businesses. This quote from one of the early participants expresses why this is such an attractive medium for young people: "Everybody feels they have some sort of talent but nowhere to express it. So it's good to be able to use your smartphone to show your talent off and have everybody recognize you" (Birtles 2016).

Valve Corporation is the creator of Steam, the world's largest digital gaming software distributor in the world. More than just a store for games, Steam has become an important community hub for players to do everything from launching their games to posting on community forums asking for technical assistance. One of the most vibrant areas of the Steam community is known as the Workshop, an area specifically designed for user-generated modifications to original games.

In this space, users can rapidly prototype everything from small tweaks to mass changes. One of the most ambitious projects currently at the Steam Workshops, for example, aims to transform *Total War: Attila* from a historical strategy game to a real-time strategy Lord of the Rings simulation. Valve Corporation understands the importance of allowing player-generated prototyping to happen and not interfere with it. After all, Valve's greatest game, *Counter Strike*, was once a user-generated modification to their original game *Half Life*. Valve's young leaders know that new products need to be released when they are good enough to get even better through input from large communities of users. The future of gaming and leadership will be shaped by youth as they enter the workforce.

CHAPTER 4

Moving Toward a Future
of Gaming for Grit

WE ARE MOVING TOWARD A WORLD WHERE YOUNG PEOPLE will bring their gaming experience to work and it will be a competitive advantage for them. Learning communities of gamers will emerge as powerful guilds to learn together, share experiences, and amplify their impact.

SURPRISE The best future leaders will be gamers.

I spoke at a CEO forum recently and introduced the idea of gaming for leadership development. After my talk, one of the CEOs from a very large company asked me: "Isn't gaming what we tell our kids *not* to do?" Jane McGonigal says is we need to be playing more games not fewer, but we may need to be playing different games. For parents, we need to go into the world of games with our kids and help them make smart choices.

As the next generation shows up for work, more of today's executives will learn the benefits of gaming—or they will be forced to retire early. Those who are 21 or younger in 2017 will have grown up with video gaming, and they will expect the sophistication of those media when they get to work.

The video gaming industry already knows that any game is exponentially better if it involves teams, a team of teams, or wider community engagement. From *Counter Strike* to *World of Warcraft* to *League of Legends*, the most successful games over the last ten years have been multiplayer focused. In these games, players must become a part of an effective team in order to achieve an objective. Even games that aren't intensely multiplayer often have a social element. Leaders in a highly uncertain world will need to game everything—in other words, they will need to explore their options in low-risk ways. The tools for doing this gameful exploration are already incredibly good and they will get even better.

Leading through gaming and guilds will make much more sense as young people join the workforce because they grew up with often very sophisticated video games and very organized and creative guilds. Massive multiplayer online role-playing games (MMORPGs), such as *World of Warcraft*, use highly customizable interfaces that allow players to quickly design experiences that are effective for both tasks and player styles. Such games are actually integrated communications platforms. When these same young players come to work, they will have sophisticated organizational skills, very high expectations, and a serious gamer mentality.

Here is my preview of what we can expect from those who are 21 or younger in 2017, those who were shaped by the threshold transformation that began in the early 2000s. I believe that those who became adults after about 2010 will be different, even though, at this point, nobody knows just how different. Figure 10 summarizes the differences that I think we will see play out over the next decade.

People used to talk about the digital divide, in which rich people had access to technology and poor people didn't. Today, no matter how poor you are—even if you're hungry and hopeless—you are likely to have access to some level of connectivity. Ten years from now, even the poorest people on the planet will have better connectivity than most people have today. Digital connectivity across the rich–poor gap will be empowering but also explosive if the gap persists.

The *Economist* published a special multi-authored report in January 2016 titled "Generation Uphill." They concluded that, globally, the younger generation is the healthiest and best educated in history. However, they are

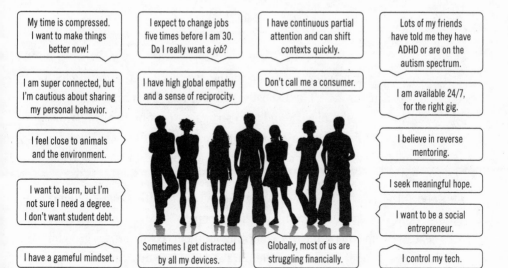

FIGURE 10 If you are 21 or younger in 2017, what are you like?
CENTER GRAPHIC BY KIRSTY PARGETER © 123RF.COM

having difficulties finding jobs, building homes, and starting families. Their elders are usually well intentioned but often don't offer much constructive hope for the next generation.

Guy Standing, a professor at the University of London, has concluded that the current economic and political pressures are creating a new economic class of young people that is characterized by insecurity and lack of any occupational identity. Professor Standing has dubbed these young people "the Precariat," and "the new dangerous class" because they don't have familiar occupational identities that tie them to places or jobs that allow them to create a positive story with their lives. Driven by desperation, anxiety, and anger—and amplified by their skills with digital media—the Precariat becomes an attractive target for dangerous affiliations with political or religious extremism (Standing 2011).

Members of the Precariat tend to

- have transient and insecure employment
- lack personal control over their own time
- be overqualified for tasks

- show uncertainty about their own work
- be well educated

In China, there is a term similar to the Precariat: the *Diaosi*, which roughly translates as *loser*. The Diaosi are mostly men born since 1980 who are serious video game players and who struggle to get by financially and socially. Their online-gaming communities are central to their lives, but they struggle to find hope for a viable future. Their futures are precarious (Candy 2017).

Robert Putnam is an American social scientist with great influence among policy makers. He studied young people in the small Ohio town where he grew up and then wrote a book about them. While he was growing up there, everyone in town used the phrase *our kids* to describe all kids in town. Our kids was an inclusive concept. When people use that label now, they are generally referring to their own kids or maybe their neighbor's kids, but not *all* kids. Many of those who society does not claim as "our kids," are, in Putnam's assessment, in deep trouble in the emerging future world (Putnam 2015).

Putnam found that the community definition of "our kids" is narrowing. However, virtual media could potentially broaden that definition, as our reach expands further to include *more* rather than fewer kids. Perhaps virtual media could help us be more inclusive.

The year 2016 saw a shift in how major video game publishers tested and marketed their games to their communities. Both Blizzard and Electronic Arts had open beta test phases that reached nearly ten million players each. These unprecedented numbers during the beta allowed for the publishers to gather crucial big data about their game before perfecting it for launch. It also gave them a unique platform to turn their potential buyers into partners by giving them a collaborative role in the process. As both games launched they quickly had large-scale communities ready and willing to buy their games. These games are now more than just a product; they are a platform for engagement, learning, and collaboration. In the future, large-scale virtual communities like these could claim many kids as their own, providing similar benefits to the inclusive communities of the past that Putnam describes.

Youth Will Blend Social Media and Gaming to Learn

Recently, Facebook partnered with Blizzard to integrate streaming capabilities so players can directly broadcast their games through Facebook. More partnerships like this will unfold over the next decade, allowing people to share their gaming experiences and become part of an extended guild or community. This kind of sharing has been common among gamers for years, but now the exchange is being formalized and even monetized through a host of sharing and hosting platforms. This makes gamers masters at a form of distributed learning and teaching that few leaders are ready for. The gaming of uncertainty will be most effective when it is done in guilds or other communities of practice that allow leaders to learn and share what they are learning.

Over the next ten years, young people will continue to drive the blending of gaming media and social media. One of the most interesting early signals of this is Twitch. With millions of gamers streaming their gameplay to the website, Twitch became the largest single community of video game streamers in the world. Some of these gamers—often professional competitive gamers—make a living entertaining communities around them. These communities tend to have strong social identities that move beyond games, evidenced by the $17,400,000 raised for charity in 2015.* Twitch shares many similarities to the innovative Chinese kids who are livestreaming a variety of different activities, sometimes for sale. However, gamers on Twitch do not need to steer too far from the formula: entertain and educate in order to benefit. Twitch viewers watch streams both to have fun and to become better gamers in their own right. In a way, Twitch streamers are ahead of the curve when it comes to gamefully engaging education and community-building efforts. Now that Twitch is owned by Amazon, it will be in a different world. Twitch the professional video gaming platform will evolve into Twitch the broader learning medium. Whether or not it succeeds commercially, it will break new ground for what I think will be a complex ecology of services and experiences that will evolve considerably beyond the original incarnation of Twitch. Even if Twitch under Amazon fails, it will fail in an interesting way.

* https://www.twitch.tv/year/2015.

The Twitch medium for learning the art of gaming has become so popular that it has already opened up creative sections where people can go and gamefully learn how to do everything from graphic design to leatherworking. Consider these live-streamers both entertainers and teachers in a gameful learning environment. In the past, your surname often designated your guild. In the future, leaders will be able to learn from many different guilds as their need for learning shifts.

In this intersection between gaming and social media we can see clear examples of how virtual guilds teach each other, prototype, and create value. I believe that leaders will have to become very good at building and maintaining these types of social networks, guilds, or whatever they come to be called in order to gamefully engage young people in work, in a hopeful way. Twitch has already done something along these lines by partnering with the estate of artist Bob Ross to stream his episodes every Monday. In a way, Bob Ross is like a guild master who is gamefully engaging other members of his distributed community, thousands at a time.

Even though I get to work with some of the most innovative organizations in the world, I have not seen a single corporation or single university that is ready for these disruptions, although there are some impressive pockets of activity. Certainly, most government agencies are not ready. The closest to being ready is the military, which uses many variations of gaming and immersive learning experiences, but even some faculty members at military graduate schools tell me that they are not well enough prepared for the next generation.

Gameful engagement will be basic to the next generation of learning, marketing, advertising, and commercials. In ten years, most rising star leaders will be gamers, with a gameful mindset. Digital natives are going to expect a much higher level of engagement as they get to work. If companies give them an experience as rich as what they've grown up with in the world of gaming and guilds, they're likely to be very productive.

Some corporations are focusing on the millennials and the changes they are bringing to the workplace. The millennials, however, are now young adults and their needs and wants are very well known. They became adults before 2010, before digital technology blossomed into media. Millennials are more digital immigrants than digital natives. Millennials are interesting and have a lot to add, but I believe those who came of age after the 2010 threshold will create the biggest disruptions and the biggest opportunities, as I discussed in the Introduction to this book. The younger they are, the more powerful their abilities will be.

I'm really optimistic about this generation of kids despite all the concerns from Standing, Putnam, and so many others—but there are definite risks. If the digital natives have little hope, some of them will be very disruptive—and even violent. But I believe that they will respond well if called up to do something important at a higher level or if they feel that it's a worthwhile cause. Calling them out won't work, but calling them up will. It's important to offer them meaningful work.

Gaming for Grit

In Chapter 3, I described how most gamers right now are gaming for resilience, the ability to be malleable and recover from stressful situations. In the future, gamers will game for more than resilience; they will game for grit. Angela Duckworth wrote the book on grit and defines it as "the tendency to sustain interest in and effort towards very long-term goals" (quoted in Candy 2017).

There is an important difference between being able to recover from sudden and stressful situations and being able to maintain an intrinsic interest in a long-term goal. Resilience will be necessary but not sufficient for the leadership demands of the future. Grit will be required to lead with hope in a world of constant disruption.

Angela Duckworth, a former McKinsey consultant and inner-city schoolteacher, writes eloquently about how extracurricular activities are one of the playing fields of grit for young children. She describes an elegant blend of motivation to have fun and to learn. Similarly many of today's games provide a blend of recreation and industry in order to focus players on goals that could take months to achieve. This definition of grit is very close to what we at Institute for the Future would describe as a good game: a story full of emotionally laden attention and gameful engagement. What will make games such a powerful learning medium will be the tendency to add high levels of grit and engagement to a traditionally stale learning method.

What ultimately ties grittiness and games together is the ability not just to recover from failure but to find value and even enjoyment in it. In the *Art of Failure*, Jasper Juut speaks about the importance of failure in games, revealing that in games, players find the unique perspective of failure and learning as enjoyment (Juut 2013). Some people are born with more grit than others, but everyone can gain grit by playing the right games—whether they are virtual or in person.

To further understand the link between grit and games, I recently read a study that demonstrated how stroke victims could rehabilitate using blended-reality games to help improve motor skill recovery. Motor skill impairment is one of most common and difficult parts of long-term stroke recovery (Saposnik 2010). Gaming for grit allowed patients to keep a more optimistic focus on their recovery.

Another study demonstrated how a group of Thai students improved their language-learning abilities by playing the multiplayer game called *Ragnarok Online*. By gaming the language-learning process students were able to improve their willingness to communicate and their overall long-term success in learning English (Reinders & Wattana 2014).

This is why I believe that gaming will be the most powerful learning medium in history. Business, government, and nonprofit agencies need to learn from the military, from pilot simulators, and from medical crisis simulations. While businesses are generally behind in their use of gaming for leadership development, the one area in business that takes advantage of gaming is public affairs. Most companies I know now game possible crisis-response scenarios that would require the corporation to respond quickly.

Gaming and guilds (or whatever they come to be called) will make this learning medium so much more powerful and so much more capable of spreading. Centralized structures will give way to distributed guilds.

In the future, we will see games move from leisurely activities to epic first-person stories that intertwine with player's lives. Gaming will provide immersive ways for people to explore and learn from the experience of others in a more effective and intimate fashion.

An extreme example is *That Dragon, Cancer*, a four-hour first-person immersive story, in which the only goal of the game is to move through the environment and interact with the story. This would seem like a simple task, but the game deals with a very emotional topic: the journey of a family as their four-year-old son struggles with cancer.

The game is a collection of voicemails, videos, recordings from doctor's visits, and emails that allow the player to be immersed in the experience. My initial thought was that this game would be an effective coping mechanism for parents going through similar situations; I was surprised that the game was popular among gamers of all ages. Many popular video game streamers shared their experience live with their communities of followers. In essence, temporary guilds were formed that allowed players to gracefully engage with some very strong emotions. The challenge for leaders will be how to evaluate and value the lessons and experiences that young people gain through gaming.

How do you learn in a VUCA world? You game.

With whom do you learn? Leaders will learn in a community with others, preferably in low-risk immersive learning experiences that allow them to prepare and practice.

Résumés Will Include Gaming Achievements

In a world where gaming becomes the most powerful learning medium in history, it will be possible for many people to move beyond just accredited degrees toward gameful preparation. The résumé of the future will include examples of game performance, with reference letters from fellow guild members or opponents.

At Institute for the Future, we have seen a few examples of this already from our job applicants. Ten years from now, résumés will most likely include a detailed gaming profile highlighting achievements across various games and platforms. Of course, prospective employers will be interested in *which* games and *what* guild members are involved.

The concept of *game achievements* in the video gaming world will become more relevant to leadership development. Game achievements recognize player's abilities and long-term exploits. Achievements carry over and can hold value across games. These achievements are part of every player's profile: they unlock bonuses, award new abilities, or simply add to the pride of playing well. The importance of achievements in games cannot be understated since they represent a player's inherited knowledge, a player's worth in virtual worlds.

Electronic Arts, for example, has put out many iterations of its popular *Battlefield* series that began with *Battlefield 1942*. Since the launch of *Battlefield 2142*, EA has experimented with a veteran system that provides seasoned *Battlefield* players with recognition of their past achievements in old *Battlefield* universes.

Similarly, the EA's *FIFA* game uses a points system that transfers with player from version to version as new iterations come out every year. This means that every game matters, even for a future in which old versions of *FIFA* are no longer relevant. This system allows players to scout out future stars, finance big-money player contracts, and improve their training efficiency based on their past *FIFA* exploits.

This notion of game achievements will carry forth into the world of work through guilds or communities of practice. In a VUCA world, leadership development will be increasingly gameful, and shared learning across games—and into real life—will become part of getting ready for work or battle, just like it is already in video games, in the military, in police work, and in firefighting.

Certainly, many young people will ask more questions about the value of higher education degrees. They will use gaming as a way of learning the skills they need and to make sense of the challenges around them. This generation has also been characterized as "generation debt" by the author Anya Kamenetz, who emphasized how difficult it is for many young people to recover from student loans or other staggering debts (Kamenetz 2006). Certainly, looming student loan debt will cause many people to seek alternative ways of learning and measuring readiness for work.

The résumé for future leaders will include the games you play and the guilds to which you belong. Figure 11 illustrates the process that leaders will follow, to practice their leadership skills in low-risk gameful worlds.

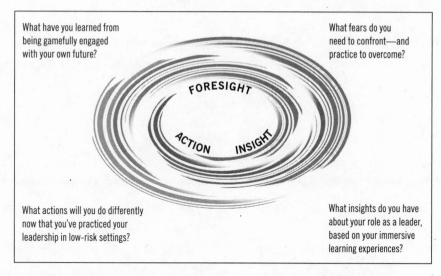

What have you learned from being gamefully engaged with your own future?

What fears do you need to confront—and practice to overcome?

FORESIGHT

ACTION   INSIGHT

What actions will you do differently now that you've practiced your leadership in low-risk settings?

What insights do you have about your role as a leader, based on your immersive learning experiences?

FIGURE 11 The new literacy of voluntary fear exposure—gaming for grit, to create readiness for a scary world

CHAPTER 5

The *New Literacy* of Leadership for Shape-Shifting Organizations

THOSE WHO ARE FLUENT IN THE NEW LITERACY OF shape-shifting organizations will say

- I am very good at leading through entangled networks that have no center, grow from the edges, cannot be controlled—and where hierarchies come and go.
- I always look for ways to create mutual-benefit partnering models for engagement.
- I seek out diverse potential partners who can help me do what I cannot do alone.

When I first came to Institute for the Future, Roy Amara introduced me to Paul Baran, one of several people who is credited with inventing packet switching, the core technology of the internet. As Paul Baran described it to me, he was asked when he was at RAND to help create a telecommunications network that would resist nuclear attack (Baran 1964). This was in the midst of the Cold War.

At that time, networks were centralized, so if an enemy attacked any portion of it, the entire network could become vulnerable. In the new architecture, instead of centralized switching, packets were separated as they were sent and then put back together again when they were delivered. Paul Baran first described this as "hot-potato routing" (Baran & Sharla 1964). But it came to be called *packet switching*, which made it possible for the network to continue working even if a portion of it was destroyed. This disruptive improvement created a new kind of network that didn't require centralized management.

Packet-switched networks have no center. They grow from the edges, and they cannot be controlled. Packet switching allows for the creation of more robust networks, but it also introduces new dilemmas of leadership. How do you lead in organizations that have no center, grow from the edges, and cannot be controlled? This question first emerged in 1972 when internet-predecessor ARPANET was publically introduced, and nobody has a clear answer yet. In the early days of packet switching, however, the concerns were more theoretical than practical. Now, packet switching and other forms of distributed computing are ready to scale.

These classic network diagrams shown in Figure 12 have been reproduced many times since Paul Baran created them. The centralized network diagram was state of the art when Baran was writing in 1964 and working to create an alternative architecture. In the Cold War, centralization had become intolerably risky. The considerable benefits of centralization were overcome by the risks of having a single target for an enemy that was becoming increasingly sophisticated in its understanding of technology.

Fast-forward 53 years to 2017 as I am writing this book. The shift from centralized to decentralized to distributed is still underway, in a very different context with much more advanced technology.

IBM recently published a visualization that looks a lot like Paul Baran's original 1964 vision of the shift from centralized to distributed, with the addition of cloud computing. In today's world, *centralized* refers to closed cloud networks that connect millions—or even billions—of devices on what is coming to be called the Internet of Things (IoT). Decentralized networks are more open, with access to a centralized cloud. Distributed networks will

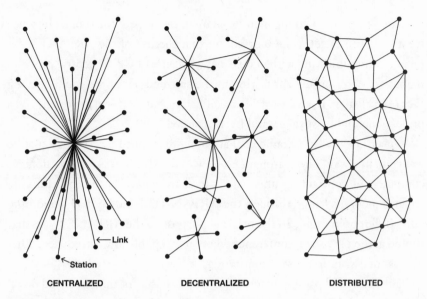

CENTRALIZED   DECENTRALIZED   DISTRIBUTED

FIGURE 12 From Paul Baran's classic 1964 paper "On Distributed Networks"

be needed to connect hundreds of billions of devices in the next generation of IoT. This shift that began in 1964 is still unfolding. While writing this book, I realized that the arc of this shift coincides with my professional career.

In 1972, I partnered with fellow Northwestern graduate student Jim Schuyler to present the results of our dissertations at the International Conference on Computer Communication at the Washington Hilton in Washington, DC, where the ARPANET was publically introduced. Jim and I had been PhD students (Jim in computer science and I in sociology of religion) together, and we were on a panel that was exploring how to use the ARPANET for interpersonal communications among scientists.*

Naïvely, I had thought that Conference on Computer Communications referred to communications among people using computer networks. I had misunderstood the title of the conference where my first big paper was accepted. Humble beginning.

---

* The other panel participants were Doug Engelbart, Murray Turoff, and Andy Lipinski.

After our panel, a young man stood up in the back of the room. His voice trembled with anger as he blurted out that the use of the ARPANET for people communicating with people was a "misuse of CPU" (central processing units). After his defiant testimony, he stormed out of the room, leaving the room cloaked in awkward silence. This was my first real experience as a professional public speaker, and I was stunned.

I never knew what became of that young man, but I now realize that he was right in a way. The reason for creating ARPANET was to allow defense computers at contracting universities to share data. Those of us thinking about human exchange through the ARPANET definitely had something quite different in mind. So the original purpose of the ARPANET was disrupted at the very same conference where it was publically introduced. That process of disruption is still continuing.

Paul Baran and packet switching, in a real sense, got things started down a path toward distributed everything. Looking to the future, I now believe that everything that *can* be distributed *will* be distributed. The obvious shift toward a digital world is becoming a less obvious shift toward a distributed one. The more digital we become, the more potential there is for distributing anything and everything.

Packet switching, brought to life in what we've come to know as the internet, will amplify distributed organizations in ways that have never before been possible. Now, more than fifty years after packet switching was invented, distributed organizations will become globally scalable. In fact, distributed organizations will become mandatory in some markets in parts of the world. Even very small organizations will be able to have very big impacts.

For example, if you are a person with extremely weird ways of thinking about the world, you will be able to find hundreds of others who have extremely weird ways of thinking that are very similar to your own. Together, the next generation web will help you amplify your shared weirdness—for good or for evil.

Over the next decade, any organization that can become distributed will become distributed. Distributed organizations will be used for both good and evil. In fact, the criminal economy and terrorist groups are disturbingly effective at using distributed organizations already.

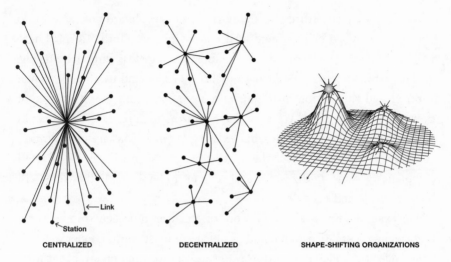

FIGURE 13 The shift from centralized to distributed

The big challenge is this: leadership for shape-shifting organizations will be really different. We do know that the overall shift will look something like Figure 13.

Clay Shirky, one of the best internet scholars, points out, "Most of the barriers to group interaction have collapsed, and without these barriers, we are free to explore new ways of gathering together and getting things done" (Shirky 2008). The internet has made possible what Shirky refers to as an "attention surplus" that—if only leaders can figure out how to refocus it and reengage it—could do things that have never been done before. Distributed organizations will be able to tap into this attention surplus more and more in the future. Shirky's powerful subtitle for *Here Comes Everybody* is a call to the future: *The Power of Organizing without Organizations.*

When he was president of Institute for the Future, Ian Morrison used to ask provocatively, "How can we have a big impact on big ideas without being big?" The models and practices for doing just that will spread virally over the next decade.

IFTF's executive director Marina Gorbis makes it clear in her book on new organizational structures that we will be able to go way beyond traditional corporate structures: "It's amazing what people are now able to do with no money, no management, and no employees" (Gorbis 2013). There will be so many new ways to have a big impact on big ideas without being big.

There are some shape-shifting organizations around us already. When I introduced this notion to friends at a large consulting company, one of them immediately said, "We *are* a shape-shifting organization!" This could be true for some consultancies, but existing organizations are only hinting at what will be possible over the next few years. A growing array of small companies is showing the way, but it remains to be seen whether they will be sustainable and scalable.

For example, Enspiral is a network of social entrepreneurship ventures that is much more distributed and nimble than most consultancies today. It runs under the following motto: "More people working on stuff that matters . . . collaboration, autonomy, transparency, diversity, entrepreneurship, non-hierarchy."* Consensys is an Ethereum blockchain development company that has a number of *spokes* (essentially projects) underway that operate like separate businesses but draw resources and tools from other spokes.** Bitcoin's core development team also functions as a shape-shifting organization where anyone can propose changes or copy the main code, but the group organically centers on a single version (van Wirdum 2016).

Automattic, the makers of Wordpress and other web services, has begun to scale as a shape-shifting organization. Wordpress.com is currently the fifth most visited web domain on the internet, despite the fact that it has only a tiny fraction of the employees of Facebook, Google, or Amazon. They describe themselves like this:

> We're a distributed company with 563 Automatticians in 56 countries speaking 78 different languages. Our common goal is to democratize publishing so that anyone with a story can tell it, regardless of income, gender, politics, language, or where they live in the world. (www.automattic.com/about/)

And of course, a range of extreme terrorist groups would qualify as shape-shifting organizations.

---

* http://enspiral.com/network-overview/.
** https://consensys.net/about/.

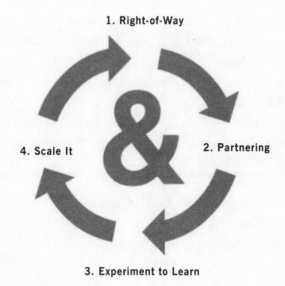

FIGURE 14 The Reciprocity Advantage Model

I believe that, over the next decade, the best organizations will be characterized by partnerships of mutual benefit, a strategy for embracing disruption with the right partners to make a company a far better leader than if they tried it alone. In a world of disruptions, mutual-benefit partnering provides a way to innovate without going it alone, to share risk, and to broaden your capabilities. Karl Ronn and I wrote a book called *The Reciprocity Advantage* in 2014 that introduced mutual-benefit partnering as a model for business growth, put it in a futures context, and provided workbook guides for how to apply this logic to your business. In this book, I am proposing how leaders can benefit from the reciprocity advantage and create a new literacy for resourceful partnering in shape-shifting organizations.

Traditional competition and centralized organizations still work in mature slow-moving markets, but rapidly changing markets will be better served by massively scalable mutual-benefit partnering. Figure 14 shows our basic model from *The Reciprocity Advantage* to help companies identify new mutual-benefit opportunities for innovation.

As we were writing *The Reciprocity Advantage*, we heard over and over again the story of the American railroads and how they missed the telecommunications revolution. These were very smart people who seemed in total control. They were referred to as the robber barons, and they included Leland Stanford. The telegraph companies approached the titans of rail-roading, so the story goes, and asked something like this: "Could we string wires over your tracks?"

The railroad people thought about it and then decided that this new connectivity would allow them to know where their trains were at any given time. The railroad and telegraph companies agreed upon a transaction that allowed the telecommunications companies to string wires over the railroad tracks. The railroads missed the fact that they weren't just in the train business. They could've been in the transportation business, but most importantly, they completely missed the telegraph business. They could've been AT&T. We asked historians how these brilliant railroad barons could have missed this opportunity.

They missed it because they loved trains too much. Also, their centralized organizational structure made it hard to see to the edges of their own businesses. Shape-shifting organizations will make this much easier, since there is no center and they grow from the edges.

Here are questions for leaders to ponder: What do you love so much about your business that you would miss a major opportunity if it moved right into your right-of-way? What do you love so much that if somebody else moves into your right-of-way you wouldn't realize it until they were too big to buy? Are you looking over the edges of your organization?

You've got to find your right-of-way: your assets, relationships, and investments that you need to run your current business in your current industry (Johansen & Ronn 2014). Underutilized assets are an important part of your right-of-way because you might be able to build on them to create new businesses. You've got to ask, whom do I have to partner with to do what I cannot do alone?

IBM has identified big data know-how as its right-of-way. That's the essence of what they're selling now. When I started my career in the 1970s, IBM was in the hardware business. They were referred to as Big Blue. While they were innovative in many ways, many people in Silicon Valley viewed them as a boring but very profitable company selling big machines. Gradually, they realized they couldn't make any money from selling hardware because hardware was becoming commoditized. Meanwhile, big data was liquefying in ways that allowed it to flow across organizations.

One of my favorite terms in Silicon Valley nowadays is *liquid data*, which means that data created in one place can flow easily to other places. The issue is not so much big data as it is big data *analytics*. There are very powerful, new ways of making sense out of data—which could mean a lot for leaders. More data and better analytics could lead to better decisions—although it also could lead to more confusion. Now that liquid data is possible, liquid leadership will become more possible. Leadership created in one place can flow to another across boundaries, what Chris Ernst called boundary-spanning leadership (Ernst & Chrobot-Mason 2010). In distributed shape-shifting organizations, we will need more liquid leadership.

Now, IBM is in the service and experiences business. It started selling services within its Smarter Planet brand, a very compelling name that draws them toward that future. Watson has now taken on this brand for the future quality for IBM. For example, IBM teamed with a very small startup company called Propeller Health, which had one product to sell: an inhaler for kids with asthma that has a GPS sensor in it. Wherever a child uses the inhaler, it tracks the location of where the spray happened. They began by mapping the use of sprays all around the larger area of Louisville. That became a big data problem: exactly where were the kids when they had trouble breathing and needed a spray? Once they figured out the patterns, they could either try to solve the air quality problem or divert the kids with asthma around the danger areas.

Once a concept like this is proven, IBM can sell the concept to any other city that has a similar challenge. That's an example of a reciprocity-based innovation strategy: IBM gave away its services in the short run, but in such a way that it could also gain business benefit in the long term. Its business success is also yielding public benefits. It's also an example of creating a new distributed organization that shares risk and rewards. Formerly centralized IBM is becoming increasingly shape-shifting IBM.

When Microsoft introduced Kinect (a gestural interface for video gaming as originally framed) in 2010, they were stunned that it was hacked within six days. Microsoft's lawyers said they would sue anyone who hacked the Kinect platform. Shortly after the lawyers' threat to sue, a prize was offered for the best hack of the Kinect platform. Two months later, Microsoft opened the platform. It has been very successful, not just as the video gaming platform alone, but also as an inexpensive gestural interface for anything. Instead of suing the hackers, Microsoft partnered with them. Now you see Microsoft in its next generation of leadership talking about organizational transformation through resourceful partnering models like this. The lesson here was not that protecting intellectual property was impossible, but that opening the platform created important business benefits. The foresight is that we are clearly moving from more closed to more open, but it will be a messy process along the way. The insight is that there will be many opportunities for mutual-benefit partnering in this increasingly open world. The actions are starting to happen, but the models for success are still to be proven.

The first night of the Major League Baseball playoffs in 2015—when Pittsburgh was playing the Chicago Cubs—I got a behind-the-scenes tour of the Major League Baseball Replay Operations Center in the Chelsea Market area of lower Manhattan in New York City. I thought I was just going to see the MLB's replay center, which is pretty interesting in itself, but it turned out we were shown something much more profound.

Major League Baseball is in the process of reimagining its right-of-way by using mutual-benefit partnering to create a novel distributed organization. It is marketing and distributing premium digital products, but not just for baseball. It started with baseball but turned into something that is going way beyond baseball. Major League Baseball Advanced Media—or MLBAM—is now distributing a wide range of premium digital assets using the same media resources that distribute baseball games to mobile devices. MLBAM covers political events, *Game of Thrones*, NCAA's Final Four, the National Hockey League, and many other events.

It is possible to imagine that ten years from now, Major League Baseball could be a business that focuses on marketing and distributing premium digital products—and just happens to play baseball on the side. The foresight is that premium digital services are becoming at least as important as content. The insight is that mutual-benefit partnering will allow new ways to share risks and rewards to create new businesses.

As we look to the future, leaders should ask this question: What is our right-of-way? In a world of shape-shifting organizations, there are many possibilities but also many potential competitors.

A right-of-way is not limited to your current core business. It could be something else that's more hidden, based on underutilized or hidden assets. We have all these challenges to our right-of-way, and as leaders we have to get really good at anticipating what that right-of-way might be, looking out to the future. You already own your right-of-way, but it may well be hidden from you in plain view. The common SWOT analysis (strengths, weaknesses, opportunities, and threats) is one tool to help you uncover it.

Leaders will all have to learn how to practice resourceful mutual-benefit partnering and how to create opportunities that benefit others, as well as themselves, in order to thrive in a world of shape-shifting organizations.

How can you protect your intellectual property if you do this? I'm not saying you have to give away core assets. Remember the partnering question I asked earlier: whom could you partner with to do what you could not do alone? It may not involve giving up your intellectual property. If you can protect your intellectual property in traditional ways, more power to you. All I am saying is that, in many industries, it's going to get harder and harder to protect your intellectual property.

Shape-shifting organizations will provide flexible ways to create business and social value.

In Silicon Valley, it used to be that, whenever you had new product discussions, it was mostly about protecting intellectual property. Now, in every new product discussion in Silicon Valley, there's always at least one lawyer at the table that says something like, "How might we create more value if we give it away?" And it isn't necessarily open source. It could be licensing. How might you make even more in return if you give it away? Since protecting intellectual property means keeping ahead of the pirates, a growing number of people are now asking, "How could we bypass the pirates by mutual-benefit partnering?"

Figure 15 is a summary of how leading shape-shifting organizations will play out over the next ten years.

The literacy of leading shape-shifting organizations will require many

Current Literacy	Future Literacy
• Leading through matrix management and hierarchical reporting chains	• Hierarchies come and go only when they add value
• Economies of scale—bigger is almost always better	• Economies of structure—reciprocity will be the currency
• Leading from the center	• Leading from the edge
• People always lead organizations	• Distributed autonomous organizations will grow

FIGURE 15 The new literacy of leading shape-shifting organizations that have no center, grow from the edges, and can't be controlled

skills, but the two most important ones are constructive depolarization and commons creation.

Leading shape-shifting organizations will amplify the need for constructive depolarization.

Constructive Depolarization: The ability to calm tense situations where differences dominate and communication has broken down and to bring people from divergent cultures toward constructive engagement

When conflict arises at the edge of organizations, leadership can become very difficult. Shape-shifting organizations can go tribal. Mutual-benefit partnering can give way to tribal warfare.

Daniel Shapiro's book *Negotiating the Nonnegotiable* presents the best practical guide I have seen to leading when distributed organizations get *too* distributed (Shapiro 2016). In the VUCA world, the potential for extreme disruption at the edges of distributed organizations is always possible. Shapiro, based on his extensive experiences in negotiation of extreme differences, highlights five "lures" that bring groups—or subsets of groups—toward what Shapiro calls "the tribal mind."

1. **Vertigo** is a warped state of consciousness in which a relationship consumes your emotional energies.

2. **Repetition compulsion** is a self-defeating pattern of behavior you feel driven to repeat.

3. **Taboos** are social prohibitions that hinder cooperative relations.

4. **Assault on the sacred** is an attack on the most meaningful pillars of your identity.

5. **Identity politics** is the manipulation of your identity for another's political benefit.

Tribes can bring people together (guilds are also a kind of tribe), but tribes get dangerous when the strength of an in-group comes at the expense of others on the outside.

Most of Shapiro's examples come from the geopolitical sphere, but as shape-shifting organizations expand, so will the challenges of leading within them—particularly with parts of the organization that are lured toward the tribal mindset and away from the collective good that the leader has in mind. The ways in which these disruptions occur will also take on new forms as shape-shifting organizations become increasingly sophisticated and the social practices become less clear.

While resisting the temptations toward tribalism, Shapiro also describes the aspirational goal of what he calls a "communal mindset," which I would think of as the cord that binds together an organization. In very practical ways, Shapiro outlines how leaders can develop a more connective way of thinking when confronted with conflicts (Shapiro 2016).

1. Uncover the mythos of identity (the personal significance of the conflict).

2. Work through emotional pain (witness, mourn, and appreciate each other's pain).

3. Build crosscutting connections (patch the organization and weave it more tightly).

4. Reconfigure the relationship (look long and envision scenarios for coexistence).

Over the next decade as shape-shifting organizations become more popular, the tensions will rise and the new digital capabilities will create weird twists that will challenge the imagination of even the best leaders. *Negotiating the Nonnegotiable* is an amazing resource for leaders of shape-shifting organizations as they strive for constructive depolarization. It provides a practical vision of what can be done to constructively depolarize situations that seem hopeless, as well as create commons spaces where assets can be created that benefit more than just individual players.

The literacy of leading shape-shifting organizations will require commons creating, which allows assets to be shared and provides mutual-benefit partnering models for innovation.

> **Commons Creation:** The ability to seed, nurture, and grow shared assets that can benefit all players—and allow competition at a higher level.

Commons creation allows leaders to share new assets that benefit more than themselves, which is required for mutual-benefit partnering. Clearly, the long-term direction is shifting from more closed to more open, but I'm not arguing that open source will prevail. Rather, in a world where everything that can be distributed will be distributed, it will be difficult to control intellectual property in traditional ways. Mutual-benefit partnering will allow companies to share risk and share rewards.

Information Technology Senior Management Forum (ITSMF) is a commons committed to the continuous professional development of black senior-level executives in the technology industry. ITSMF provides an instant community for African Americans in the mostly white world of information technology professionals. Its mission is to increase the representation of black professionals at senior levels in technology and to impact organizational innovation and growth by developing and nurturing dynamic leaders through enrichment of the mind, body, and soul. The forum also offers a management academy for mid-level rising star leaders and an executive academy focused on preparing future CIOs and other top executives with technology specialties. Emerge is an ITSMF program focused on women of color.

ITSMF is a distributed organization with a strong future orientation and a strong clarity statement of its mission: "By 2020, ITSMF will graduate 500 professionals through a series of rich, developmental, and career-advancing programs, and do so by being a second family to its members and partners."*

ITSMF also stands for another meaning that expresses its goal: It's My Family. It is a commons that provides value for African American leaders as they enter and grow their careers in the IT field, but it is also a commons for the corporations who fund and benefit from it. Shape-shifting organizations are becoming increasingly common and increasingly diverse. What they share in common is the ability to distribute authority and move beyond traditional centralized ways of organizing.

* www.itsmfonline.org.

CHAPTER 6

Moving Toward a Future of Distributed Authority

IN THE NEAR FUTURE, MANY TRADITIONAL HIERARCHI-cal structures will bend and break. Lots of diverse partners will come together in new ways to create new kinds of organizational structures that will be more fluid and less rigid. While this will feel like a radically new future, and in some ways it is a radically new future, there are deep roots in the past. The future that is about to happen has been brewing for a very long time.

SURPRISE Almost nothing happens that is truly new.

Most things we think are new are not really new. Almost everything that happens was tried and failed years before—often in Silicon Valley. My advice: don't ask, "What's new?" because if something is truly new, it almost certainly won't happen any time soon. Rather, you should be asking, "What's ready to take off?"

Distributed organizations are now ready to take off and scale globally.

"We tend to over-
estimate the impact of
technology in the short
term and underestimate
in the long term."

—Roy Amara
Institute for the Future

FIGURE 16 Amara's Law

When I first came to Silicon Valley, I was hired at Institute for the Future by Roy Amara, the president and father of what has become known in the futures field as Amara's Law. (See Figure 16.) Others have said similar things, but as far as I know, Roy was the first to say it.

The job of leaders is to have the perspective necessary to recognize true innovation and when it is ready to take off. Amara's Law tempers short-term enthusiasm, but it fuels long-term hope. Amara's Law can help leaders develop the perspective necessary to understand when the timing is right for important disruptions to occur. The capability to connect distributed organizations was made possible by the invention of packet switching. Over the next decade these capabilities will finally be able to spread on a global scale.

I like to think of a shape-shifting organization as a fishnet lying on a dock. (See Figure 17.) Each node represents a potential leader. If you pick up one node, a temporary hierarchy forms with a temporary leader. Pick up another node, another temporary hierarchy forms with another leader. Hierarchies come and go as needs arise. Leadership is distributed and var-ied. Such shape-shifting organizations are both strong and flexible, like a fishnet. Digital networks are like the cord on the fishnet.

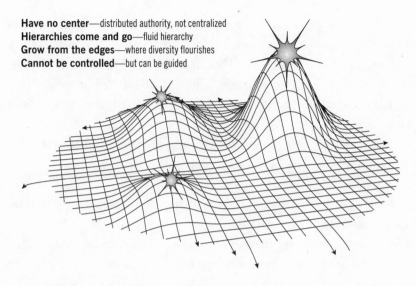

Have no center—distributed authority, not centralized
Hierarchies come and go—fluid hierarchy
Grow from the edges—where diversity flourishes
Cannot be controlled—but can be guided

FIGURE 17 Shape-shifting organizations

I first suggested the notion of a fishnet organization in a book called *Upsizing the Individual in the Downsized Organization* that I did with novelist Rob Swigart in 1994—right about the time that the World Wide Web was just taking off. In 1994, we anticipated the fishnet organization this way:

> The fishnet is a metaphor we have carefully chosen to express the form of organization emerging from the current turmoil. If we are correct that tomorrow's organizations will look and function like fishnets, then it is important to think of them, talk about them, and create them like fishnets. If we hire pyramid builders or mechanics or road builders to create an organizational fishnet, the results will be disappointing. Fishnets are not made of wood, stone, steel, or concrete for a reason. Unfortunately, people who think they are building rigid structures, not fishnets, are still building many of today's corporate organizations. Their metaphors, and therefore their tools, are wrong. (Johansen and Swigart 1994)

The shift toward fishnet organizations has happened more slowly than we forecast in 1994, and I've concluded that the term *fishnet organization* is more confusing than helpful. Instead, I'm now using the term *shape-shifting organizations*. I see now that Rob and I fell into the Amara's Law trap: we overestimated the impact of this new form of organization in the short term and thought it would happen more quickly than it has. Still, we are on track for long-term impacts—which will become apparent over the next decade. Now is the time to prototype new kinds of distributed shape-shifting organizations—whatever they come to be called—and learn how to lead through them.

Over the next decade shape-shifting organizations will become much more common, and distributed leadership will become mandatory—even though the literacy of distributed leadership is still very much a work in progress. Shape-shifting organizations will disrupt traditional organizations and, in some cases, blend with them.

I believe that shape-shifting organizations will be part of a larger economic shift that I noticed some time ago but will become obvious over the next decade:

> In the topsy-turvy world of teams and teams of teams, economies of scale are giving way to economies of structure. . . . Now, the structure a company creates for itself, its flexibility and responsiveness, shapes its ability to adapt and thrive. Just being bigger is not enough. Size is only a virtue when it is combined with flexibility. (Johansen & Swigart 1994)

Economies of structure—organizational structure—will be required to thrive in the world of the increasingly VUCA future. Shape-shifting organizations will be more messy but more productive than traditional organizations.

Stan Davis, author of the seminal book *Future Perfect* and the inventor of the term *mass customization*, did an endorsement blurb for our *Upsizing* book that nicely frames the organization of the future and the upsized people who will lead them:

> There is nobody at the helm of the corporate ship because there is no helm. Managers do have an effect, but they are pulling and rearranging fishnets . . . in the fishnet organization, being in the center is the last place you want to be. This is the dead zone, where innovation, excitement, and rewards are lacking. Those things exist at the edges . . . those at the edges have taken responsibility for their own lives. They are the upsized individuals. The future is theirs. (Johansen & Swigart 1994)

Wave 1: Data exchange

Wave 2: Scientific communications exchange

Wave 3: Information retrieval from central source

Wave 4: Enterprise management

Wave 5: Scalable interpersonal communities

Now...Wave 6: Decentralized business match-making for value exchange

———— FORESIGHT: Faster transformation from tools to media ————

Next...Wave 7: Value exchange without central authority

FIGURE 18 The evolution of internet disruption

Shape-shifting organizations will become more common as the much more distributed next generation of the internet accelerates.

The 1972 public announcement of the ARPANET at the Washington Hilton introduced the first wave of digital disruption I have seen and experienced during my professional career. Certainly, some waves overlapped, and the exact dates for each wave are debatable—even in retrospect. More importantly, these were not separate disruptions; they were combinatorial.*

To make things even more difficult to understand, some of these innovations were neither planned nor orchestrated. What actually happened was often quite different from what was intended.

Figure 18 shows the waves of disruption the way that I experienced them, moving from where we've been to where we are to where we are going. I have a unique perspective on this evolution, since my career arc follows the

---

* *Combinatorial innovation* is a term I first heard from Hal Varian (UC Berkeley and Google). Combinatorial innovation is not new, but it is certainly intensifying. The key point is that innovations are not isolated, but rather, mixed in ways that are often impossible to understand in advance.

evolution of the internet: I finished my PhD in 1972 and was at a conference where the ARPANET was publicly introduced. While I'm not a digital native, I had my first internet identity in 1973 when I joined Institute for the Future.

Notice that Wave 7 will make shape-shifting organizations and economies of organization practical and scalable, *finally*. Wave 7 will make possible a variety of new paths toward distributed everything.

What's Next: The Blockchain Disruption

In the language of 2017, Wave 7 will grow out of a conversation that includes blockchain, an emerging digital paradigm that is taking shape at the edges of the internet. Shape-shifting organizations and new economies of organization will be created using blockchain or similar platforms for distributed computing.

When Institute for the Future opened its new Blockchain Futures Lab in 2016, here is how people were thinking about blockchain as it started to take shape:

> After incubating through more than a million Bitcoin transactions and a host of next-generation developer projects, it is now on the tips of tongues of CEOs and CTOs, startup entrepreneurs, and even governance activists. Though these stakeholders are beginning to understand the disruptive potential of blockchain technology and are experimenting with its most promising applications, few have asked a more fundamental question: What will a world driven by blockchain technology look like a decade from now? (IFTF 2016)

After the first expert workshop, the Blockchain Futures Lab revised its vision a bit to conclude that blockchain is an immature but rapidly evolving technology that will disrupt not only business models but also the social and political fabric. In some ways, it is an inherently political technology, since it pushes everything out of the center. It is a tool for both efficient coordination and disruption.

Think of blockchain as distributed computing that can track the status of autonomous virtual objects and provide security *without central authority*.

It is being used to prototype new infrastructure for organizing ourselves in a global society.

In the future, blockchain will be

- a way to provide high-trust interactions in low-trust environments
- a way of documenting and verifying integrity
- a new kind of coordination being built on top of the internet
- a distributed unchangeable ledger or log of information that tells an immutable story of provenance

Blockchain will provide the advantages of a single platform without the disadvantages of a single provider, like Google, Facebook, or Twitter. It will be to value what today's internet is to information.

It is a big step toward distributed everything. Although it will surely be a confusing process of creation, blockchain will make it possible for shape-shifting organizations and economies of organizations to thrive. Also, blockchain will challenge traditional organizations in profound ways.

Blockchain will be a critical infrastructure for the future, although it may not be called blockchain. Indeed, some new systems are being called blockchain, even if they don't involve blocks or chains. Such difficulty in naming an emerging technology blob on the horizon is typical of the emerging technologies I have studied in my career. If you get the name of a new technology right, it draws you toward the future. World Wide Web and internet, for example, were very good names. If you get the name of a new technology wrong, you fight it as you move toward the future. Artificial intelligence is the worst name of any new technology I've studied. The name blockchain isn't bad, but it doesn't highlight what this new technology will be used for and what sorts of functional outcomes will become possible. Distributed computing infrastructure such as blockchain will empower diversity.

Shape-Shifting Organizations Will Be Diverse Organizations

When I first began my career in the 1970s, I understood calls for diversity as calls for social equity and social justice. Now, while these are still issues, the calls for diversity are more likely to be calls for innovation.

Scott Page is a professor of complex systems, political science, and economics at the University of Michigan and the Santa Fe Institute. His book called *The Difference* makes a strong case that diversity leads to better outcomes. Diversity, for Scott Page, includes diverse perspectives, diverse interpretations, diverse heuristics, and diverse predictive models.

> Almost by definition, breakthroughs require serendipity. That serendipity arises from diverse preparedness. It derives from someone noticing and knowing how to interpret strange phenomena. Albert Einstein wrote that "the most beautiful thing we can experience is the mysterious. It is the source of all true art and science." In trying to come to grips with those mysteries, we apply our tools. The more tools we amass through training, refine by experience, and filter through our identities, the better. (Page 2007)

Shape-shifting organizations grow from the edges, and it is at the edges where diversity and innovation thrive. Shape-shifting organizations will create a radical increase in the potential for serendipity and mysterious opportunity—if only we are on the lookout for it.

Ten years ago, most interesting tech signals came from the developed countries in general and Silicon Valley in particular. Now some of the most interesting signals I see are coming from Africa. Even though the infrastructure is often crude, the innovation spirit is very developed, and amazingly creative things are happening with the development of applications using simple technology. What has happened is that there is less of a digital divide. Now, no matter how poor you are, you have some access to connectivity. If you look ten years ahead, it is going to be even better connectivity. Corporations are rethinking the role of diversity. It is still true that rich people have access to better tech, but poor people—even if they are hungry, homeless, and hopeless—have access to some tech. Their connectivity and power will increase over the next decade. Diversity will fuel innovation.

Bright Simons, the founder of M-Pedigree (which uses text message scratch codes to reduce the risk of pharmaceutical counterfeiting), describes the role of African technology and innovation in an increasingly global world.

It [African innovation] has a dirty little secret: it is inherently global in nature. Innovation wants to be global. . . . True innovation wants to fly away, to intermix, to mongrelize, to become impure, to lose its way, to find its mojo again, to bless, to be damned, to be redeemed. True innovation happens in Africa. True innovation happens in the African Diaspora. True innovation happening outside Africa is sometimes championed by Africans. It is a complex picture, and that is a good thing. And that is my point. Africa is becoming a site for global innovation, and Africans are contributing to innovation globally, and that is as it should be. (Kirshbaum 2013)

The Need for Clarity in Shape-Shifting Organizations

Leaders of shape-shifting organizations will need great clarity about where they want the organization to go, but great flexibility about how they might get there. In the military, as I mentioned earlier, this kind of leadership style is called commander's intent. I call it *clarity*.

The military is certainly ahead of business in understanding how to lead shape-shifting organizations. In addition to commander's intent, the Navy uses a practice called UNODIR, which is also described as command by negation. Basically, it means that a leader sends a message to superiors saying something like "I will do this unless you say I should do something different."

In practice, the doctrine is built around the idea that individual ship commanders or officers will be allowed to undertake autonomous operations. In exchange, they report their intention to do so to their superior officer, noting that the action will be taken UNODIR (UNless Otherwise DIRected) and provide a continual stream of information to the superior officer, who is not required to sign off on the plan or execute it, but gets involved only if the superior objects. Command by negation is the override that allows superior officers to step in if they take issue with the plan, but otherwise allows the subordinate officer to operate as he or she sees fit.

The primary advantage of command by negation is that the doctrine frees up leaders to look at the bigger picture; unlike in traditional naval warfare, they are no longer required to actively coordinate the actions of each vessel or unit under their command. In addition, it allows individual commanding officers closer to the ground, who have a better sense of the tactical position, to operate autonomously and contribute to the task force's overall actions.

Another military practice that helps leaders lead shape-shifting organizations and create economies of organization is the After Action Review. As I described in Chapter 3, the basic principle behind AARs is to use every experience in the field as a learning opportunity. In my experience working with the Army War College and other parts of the military, AARs are built into the way that leaders lead every day. Such a learn-as-you-go mentality will become increasingly necessary as ideas scatter across global networks. Discerning patterns of connection will become a critical leadership skill. Our knowledge media will expand even further in the world of distributed computing.

It was Mark Stefik from Xerox PARC in 1986 who seeded a provocative conversation on what he then called "the next knowledge medium." In his groundbreaking paper, he built on the core notion of memes:

> Memes are carried by people. They are knowledge units that are transmitted in conversations and that are contained in minds. Memes can be reinterpreted in new environments and expressed in new combinations.... In the meme model, a carrier is an agent that can remember a meme and communicate it to another agent. People are meme carriers and so are books. However, there is an important difference: People can apply knowledge, whereas books can only store it. (Stefik 1986)

Leaders create memes, respond to memes, build on memes, and fight memes. Leaders in shape-shifting organizations of the future will trade in memes. They will fuel communication—and miscommunication—for shape-shifting organizations. News and fake news will spread via memes.

Some memes will spread like wildfires through shape-shifting organizations. My colleague Jeremy Kirshbaum looks for memes that

- are a single act, or related series of acts, that link to some larger story
- happen in a public place, or at least a place that is important to an organization

- are dramatically discontinuous in a compelling way
- spread quickly to a larger conversation*

Leaders in shape-shifting organizations will be very good at seeding and steering wildfire events and the memes that hover above them. While leaders in shape-shifting organizations cannot just tell people what to do, they can create or build on dramatic events that compel people to act.

The early experiences with wildfire memes are wildly mixed. Terrorist groups have used them to terrorize people, such as recording beheadings and sharing them widely over social media for recruiting. On the other hand, the Ice Bucket Challenge was a wildfire meme that raised an incredible amount of money in a very short time for a wonderful cause, the ALS Foundation. The rapid spread of the Pokémon Go game is another example. Black Lives Matter is a particularly powerful meme tied to a larger movement for social justice. Wildfire memes like these cannot be controlled, but they can be seeded, fueled, and steered—though not in ways that traditional command-and-control leaders understand.

A different kind of wildfire meme flamed up in May of 2016 when a new organization called The DAO was crowdfunded and brought to life. Its bylaws were written in code, and it was authorized to act as a single economic entity (the usual definition of a corporation), but it was not yet recognized by any governmental entity. It was given its authority through the computer-coded agreements built into the blockchain: "The DAO is a paradigm shift in the very idea of an economic organization. It offers complete transparency, total shareholder control, unprecedented flexibility, and autonomous governance" (Bannon 2017).

The DAO was a signal from the future, even though it was essentially a failure in the present. In true Silicon Valley fashion, it failed in an interesting way. In the future world of distributed computing, it will become possible to create distributed autonomous corporations (what are starting to be called DACs) with no people. Consider the possibility of an Uber-like ride service without a human corporation behind it. Riders could find drivers

---

* These basic characteristics were first articulated by my colleague Jeremy Kirshbaum in a project we were doing together.

without a central company as the go-between. An algorithm, rather than a corporation in the traditional sense, could match riders with drivers, or riders with driverless cars. Over the next decade, DACs will become practical.

The company called The DAO, a kind of DAC, was a distributed venture capital fund with no central manager. The plan was that DAO token holders would vote to decide what projects to fund. In its initial funding round, it raised the equivalent of over 150 million USD. The DAO collapsed without ever funding a project, however.

Some people say the collapse was because it was illegally hacked, but this was not strictly true. One user of the platform did divert significant amounts of money for personal benefit, but not by exploiting security weaknesses in the code. Instead, this investor used the rules of the platform in an unintended way. So it was not necessarily thievery, but it certainly wasn't playing the game in the way it was intended. The technology worked perfectly, but the social practices did not.

The DAO came to life on the Ethereum blockchain. Vitalik Buterin, the founder of Ethereum, said colorfully:

> Whereas most technologies tend to automate workers on the periphery doing menial tasks, blockchains automate away at the center. Instead of putting the taxi driver out of a job, blockchain puts Uber out of a job and lets the taxi driver work with the customer directly. (Tapscott & Tapscott 2016)

Buterin uses the term *DAO* generically (as distinguished from the company called The DAO which I describe above), and he defines it as "an entity that lives on the internet and exists autonomously, but also heavily relies on hiring individuals to perform certain tasks that the automation itself cannot do" (Buterin 2014).

Ian Maya Panchèvre, a political theorist who studied at Yale and currently works at Intuit, provides an overall assessment of blockchain and its prospects in his paper called intriguingly "Techno-Tyranny: Introducing the Decentralized Autonomous Organization."

> As a "value protocol," the blockchain is vastly superior to any preceding system, including the "communication protocol" known as the internet. In theory, the blockchain can be repurposed to issue, store, and exchange

any sort of digital asset, not just currency. Medical records, software licenses, stock certificates, car keys, real estate titles, domain names, copyrights, political votes, and nuclear launch codes represent a fraction of the potential use cases to which a blockchain may be applied. (Panchèvre 2015)

Panchèvre begins his paper with a term coined by political theorist Hannah Arendt: *rule by nobody*. Arendt was referring originally to government bureaucracies that could become tyrannical and unaccountable because there was no single person at the center. Panchèvre makes the case that this fear will become much more tangible as DAOs become more powerful. On the other hand, algorithms may prove to be even more productive—or even more human—than some human-run companies.

In the past, most people thought of automation as starting with menial tasks at the fringes of organizations. However some new forms of distributed computing will automate from the center. The basic rules and operations of the company could be embedded into the code, including some top-level decision making. This does *not* remove the need for leadership, however. The operational aspects of leadership decrease, but the inspirational and social aspects increase. Memes will drive the organization, and leaders will carry and trade in memes. Leadership will become more important but less prescribed.

The practices and processes of leadership will be prototyped over the next decade. Certainly, there will be failures like the DAO, but there will be successes as well. The memes of distributed organizations will spread rapidly, and the models for success—and failure—are beginning to mount.

Shape-Shifting Organizations Will Be Difficult to Lead

I met Dee Hock in the 1990s, well after he had founded Visa International and well after he invented much of the credit card system as we know it today. After recovering from a bruising experience as the founder and first CEO of Visa, Dee Hock concluded that Visa was a prototype for a new form of organization that is similar to what I'm now calling a shape-shifting organization. Dee Hock called it a *chaord*, for part chaos and part order. He said that the internet was the first chaordic organization and Visa International was the second. Here's how he defined a chaord:

1. Any self-organizing, self-governing, adaptive, nonlinear, complex organism, organization, community, or system, whether physical, biological or social, the behavior of which harmoniously blends characteristics of both chaos and order. 2. An entity whose behavior exhibits observable patterns and probabilities not governed or explained by the rules that govern its constituent parts . . . patterned in a way dominated neither by chaos or order. 3. Characteristic of the fundamental organizing principles of evolution and nature. (Hock 1999)

Leaders in chaordic organizations decide when to play which card: chaos or order.

When his book *Birth of the Chaordic Age* came out, Dee Hock sent me a signed copy with a personal note that said in part: "Whether it will attract enough attention to help catalyze the kind of institutional change that a livable world seems to demand is impossible to know, but one can always hope."

The *Birth of the Chaordic Age* did not succeed the way Dee Hock had hoped. He formed the Chaordic Alliance to help seed, nurture, and spread the concept. The Alliance lasted for about five years but eventually folded. I've tried to discern just what happened, and I suspect it was mostly about timing. Also, I never thought the term *chaord* was very compelling, though it did express the essence of the new form of organization that is still emerging. Dee Hock did very interesting things at the birth of shape-shifting organizations, but he wasn't able to help them scale. In fact, he wasn't even able to create a sustainable organization at Visa International, which is now a rather traditional company—far from the bold vision of its founder.

There are new models emerging, particularly from experiences in the military, which is ahead of business in learning how to organize in a VUCA world. For example, Stanley McChrystal (retired U.S. Army general) has a fascinating book called *Team of Teams: New Rules of Engagement for a Complex World.* McChrystal emphasizes connectivity, idea flow, and trust as key to creating shape-shifting organizations:

"Idea flow" is the ease with which new thoughts can permeate a group. Pentland [Professor Alex Pentland from MIT] likens it to the spread of the flu: a function of susceptibility and frequency of interaction. The key to increasing the "contagion" is trust and connectivity between otherwise separate elements of an establishment. The two major determinants of idea flow, Pentland has found, are "engagement" within a small group like a team, a department, or a neighborhood, and "exploration"—frequent contact with other units. In other words a *team of teams*. (McChrystal 2015)*

Nobody can predict what these new forms of organizations will be called. *Team of teams* is a possibility, and McChrystal provides practical field advice about success. I like the term *shape-shifting organizations* better, but nobody can predict what term will stick as these new forms of organizing scale. But there will be cautionary tales, along with the promise.

Some distributed organizations will be sinister. Daniel Suarez's frightening thriller called *Daemon* captures this potential better than any other book I've ever read. The *Chicago Sun-Times* cover blurb sets the tone: "*Daemon* does for surfing the web what *Jaws* did for swimming in the ocean." *Daemon* describes a world where a deceased and demented video game designer leaves behind him a shape-shifting organization of terror. It had no center, it grew from the edges, and it definitely was not able to be controlled:

Our monitoring resulted in several dozen arrests, but the Daemon network is massively parallel—no one person or event is critical to its survival. It has no ringleaders and no central point of failure. And no central repository of logic. None of the Daemon's agents knows anything more than a few seconds in advance, so informants have been useless. It also seems highly adept at detecting monitoring. (Suarez 2009)

The future of distributed organizations will be daemonic, with a wild puzzling mix of good, great, and evil. The currency of distributed organizations will be reciprocity, or mutual-benefit partnering.

Figure 19 on the next page shows the process that leaders will need to follow to develop their abilities to lead shape-shifting organizations.

---

* This quote in McChrystal's book draws from Alex Pentland, *Social Physics: How Good Ideas Spread: The Lessons from a New Science* (New York: Penguin, 2014), pages 19–20 and 33–34.

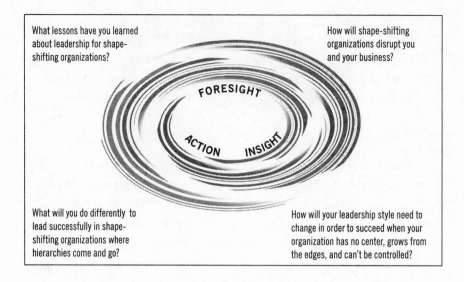

What lessons have you learned about leadership for shape-shifting organizations?

How will shape-shifting organizations disrupt you and your business?

FORESIGHT

ACTION　INSIGHT

What will you do differently to lead successfully in shape-shifting organizations where hierarchies come and go?

How will your leadership style need to change in order to succeed when your organization has no center, grows from the edges, and can't be controlled?

FIGURE 19 The new literacy of leading shape-shifting organizations that have no center, grow from the edges, and can't be controlled—while hierarchies come and go

CHAPTER 7

The *New Literacy* of Being There When You Are Not There

THOSE WHO ARE FLUENT IN THE LITERACY OF BEING there when you are not there will say

- I am skilled in the use of multiple media as I communicate my leadership, including not only in-person meetings but also a wide range of electronic media.
- I am skillful in choosing which medium is good for what, with whom.
- I am able to communicate my leadership presence continuously, even when I am not physically present.

We all need some fresh thinking about meetings. Comedian Dave Barry captured the cynicism that most people have about in-person business meetings: "If you had to identify, in one word, the reason why the human race has not achieved, and never will achieve, its full potential, that word would be 'meetings'" (Brainyquote 2016).

Dictionary.com defines *meeting* as "the act of coming together." I like that definition, but I think that meetings also involve the *process* of planning and gathering, not just the *act* of meeting in person—as well as the process of follow-up activities that should come out of most meetings.

The seventh definition for *meeting* in Dictionary.com is "a place or point of contact; junction; union." I like that definition even better, and it applies directly to what leaders will need to do in the increasingly distributed future. Leaders will need to find new points of contact in the distributed organizations within which they will be working. Leaders will need a new leadership presence, through a wide mix of media and in-person meetings in varied combinations. Leaders will need to create organizational cultures that are amplified by the increasingly rich mix of media options that will emerge over the next decade. Today's smart phones and tablets will look quaint a decade from now. Those leaders who think they are in a futuristic world of telework now will be shocked by what is coming. Even when leaders are not present in person, they will need to have their presence felt. This has always been true, but it will be increasingly important in shape-shifting organizations. The good news is that the tools for culture seeding and nurturing will be so much better than what we have today. Augmented reality, mixed reality, and virtual reality are the current buzzwords for a new blended-reality world of work that will take shape over the next decade.

Most leaders I know today are at their best when they are there physically, in person as we say. When they are not present physically, however, there is often a big gap. Many leaders I know are not very good in conference calls, video conferencing, social media, or other forms of electronic media for staying in touch. They are varied in their abilities—once they get away from in-person presence—skewing toward pretty bad. Most don't have much multimedia presence. If you have your own multimedia flair, you can be a much stronger leader even if you're not there physically.

In a world of disruptions, leaders will need to have a presence at all times, anyplace, anytime. Sometimes, they will need to feel present everyplace, every time—without feeling intrusive. Leaders will need to make very smart decisions about when to travel and when to use which virtual medium in what way with whom.

I have been working with senior executives for more than thirty years now, and my sense is that many of them travel too much and they travel at the wrong times. Certainly, some of today's leaders—especially the younger ones—use today's virtual media very well. In the future, leaders will need to be very skilled at communicating their leadership through multiple media.

When I started studying teleconferencing and social media in the 1970s, most systems designers assumed that meeting face-to-face was the ideal medium for human communication. The (often-unstated) goal in those days was to design an electronic medium that came as close as possible to meeting face-to-face. However, we should be able to do better than using new technology to replicate what we did before. In-person meetings will continue to be best for certain things, but electronic media should allow us to go beyond the ways that we meet today.

I used video teleconferencing for the first time in the mid-1970s. The video wasn't very good and the audio was worse, but the goal was to get as close to a face-to-face meeting as possible. The design vision of today's system still seems to be grounded in an unexamined assumption that in-person meetings are the ultimate form of human communication. This old-fashioned belief is that the closer virtual meetings can replicate in-person meetings, the better.

Rather than designing virtual systems to simulate being there, I think we should be designing to be *better* than being there. Being there in-person is great for orientation, trust building, and renewal, but in a world of ambient communications technology, leaders will have a new set of challenges that will go beyond simulating in-person meetings.

As you think about whether or not in-person meetings are the optimal for communicating your leadership, consider this reflection from George Martin, the producer of the Beatles:

> When I joined EMI... the criterion by which recordings were judged was their faithfulness to the original. If you made a recording that was so good that you couldn't tell the difference between the recording and the actual performance, that was the acme. And I questioned that. I thought, OK, we're all taking photographs of an existing event. But we don't have to make a photograph. We can paint. And that prompted me to experiment. (Obituary, *New York Times* 2016)

I recognized the George Martin disruption when I first heard the Beatles album *Sgt. Pepper's Lonely Hearts Club Band,* which may not have been *better* than being at a Beatles concert, but it certainly was *beyond* in a startling way.

The world of leadership at a distance hasn't gone through that kind of transformation yet. I'm hoping that the George Martin of virtual media for organizations will arrive soon.

In the future world, leaders will need to develop their own brand of blended-reality presence. New media will provide much more powerful ways to create organizational culture—beyond just good meetings. I think that the kids will be a big help, if their parents don't slow them down.

Many of today's parents have an understandable but largely inaccurate nostalgia about how wonderful in-person conversations between kids and their parents used to be before smart phones. Parents are understandably worried about their kids staring at their phones instead of talking to each other in person. There is no way back, however, to the pre–smart phone, pre–social media world. I'm sure that there were many wonderful conversations in the days before smart phones, but we don't want to fall into a backward-looking—and ultimately futile—attempt to try to make conversations great again. Rather, we should look forward into the new blended-reality world that will include great communication through a wide range of media—including in-person conversations.

Meeting in person will be crucial, but in the context of a blended-reality and increasingly distributed world. We should all be focused on creating great conversations in a multimedia world. For parents, this means listening to and learning from your kids, as well as providing them the wisdom they need to create great conversations, whatever the medium. In general, kids are likely to be better multimedia communicators (even if they do need help in person) and better gamers, but adults—because of our age—have license to play the wisdom card. We have the bigger picture, but we also need reverse mentoring.

The basic options for meeting involve time (simultaneous or spread out over time) and place (same place, or some mix of locations). Figure 20 is a map that shows the blend of options that every leader must consider.

To me, it is obvious that we have to rethink the basic idea of a *meeting.* We

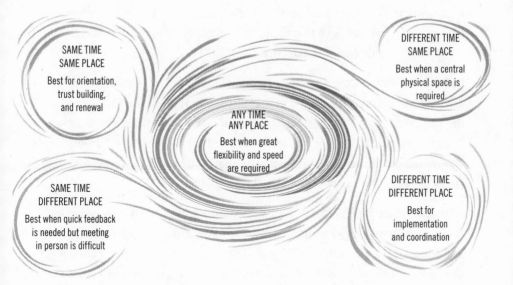

FIGURE 20 The blend of options that every leader must consider

need to create rich cultures of communication that include a wide array of media options. The most basic meeting option that most of us think about is same time/same place, an in-person meeting, typically in a conference room or an office or a coffee shop. At the other extreme is different time/different place, a meeting spread out over both time and distance. Most social media communications fit here.

Same time/different place could be a conference call or video teleconference or some form of web meeting like WebEx or Google Hangout. Finally, different time/same place could be a team room, a "war room," a factory floor, a trader's room where markets are followed globally, or even an office where people are there at varied times yet all work together. Increasingly as mobile technology improves and as more organizations work across multiple time zones, leaders need to work any time/any place.

Each leader will need to develop a personal communications strategy and style that matches with the range of meeting options across time and distance. Great leaders will not only be trained in a wide range of media, but they will also have their own signature flair within each medium. At this stage, the media options are improving rapidly, and the styles of use are still taking shape. As I have worked with these media and seen a wide range of leaders use them, I believe that the media mix options for leaders will break down into roughly into five categories.

Same Time/Same Place: Best for getting to know others, developing trust, and understanding context and cultural background of others. Also, meeting in person is best for periodic renewal for people working together at a distance over time so they can reconnect and recharge their relationships. **Downsides:** All have to be present simultaneously; only one person can speak at once; it requires physical meeting spaces.

Different Time/Different Place: Best for coordination of tasks and working fast—all of which work much better if workers have a shared orientation and sense of trust in advance. In global work situations, time zone separation makes it difficult to work simultaneously, so asynchronous media are required. **Downsides:** It's difficult to stay in synch across time and distance. It's sometimes difficult to reach closure. Because immediate correction may not be possible, there is a greater potential for misunderstood comments being offensive. An upsetting comment can lead others to stew with no resolution. Trust can wane.

Same Time/Different Place: Best when coordination and quick feedback is needed and it is important to get a "sense of the meeting," but it is not possible to get together in person for some reason. Simultaneity can make it easier to reach closure and communicate urgency, as well as to keep things rolling. **Downside:** Everyone has to be present simultaneously, which is often difficult to schedule—especially across time zones.

Same Place/Different Time: Best when a central location or physical space is required for the work tasks, but being at the space simultaneously is either not possible or not required. **Downside:** Physical space is limited.

Any Time/Any Place: Best for continuous communication and staying in touch. **Downside:** Over-connection can lead to an unthinking interrupt-driven always-on style of communication.

Each leader needs his or her own personal strategy for each media option, as well as a personal skills development plan. Even though I work with great companies, I don't often see leadership development programs that include this kind of learning. The human resources function should be offering such programs as part of leadership and executive development. These options should blend together in a palette of communications options to match the style of each leader. Social media presence, by today's definition of social media, will not be enough. Today's social media are not powerful enough to support the world of shape-shifting organizations. As I discussed in Chapters 1 and 2, you need to look ten years ahead and then work backward. There is too much noise in the present to get a clear view.

Each leader will need a personal multimedia flair, but that doesn't necessarily mean using the latest technology. Rather, it means clever use of the media that you have and matching it to your own personal style and work needs.

This is the challenge for leaders: How can you lead without being there? How you present your leadership will vary a lot. Today we have a limited mix of media options, but tomorrow, leaders will lead in a media-rich world. This chapter is all about the next generation of groupware, but we no longer need to call it that.

All leaders will have to be digitally savvy enough to make good media choices and to use the media well. The blended-reality world is moving fast. It is already too late to catch up—but it's a great time to leapfrog.

Even if a leader is sleeping, his or her cloud of intelligent agents should be working constantly. All leaders will have a cloud of resources and filters working for them at all times. Everyone will have their own cloud, with options that involve which filters you use and what kind of interface you choose. Today's laptops, tablet computers, and smart phones will look clunky in this future world. The interface will be gestural, graceful, and embedded in how we live, work, and lead.

Leaders moving around in the physical world will choose what they want to see and how they want to see it. You may be more open to outside stimuli, but someone else could be more closed. As we are walking down the street, any of us will be able to say, "I don't even like this street, I'm going to filter it to look the way I want it to look." Depending on which filter we choose, we might see the homeless guy and help him, or we may edit him out of our view. It's really up to us.

Current Literacy	Future Literacy
• In-person presence is the most important aspect of leadership.	• Leadership from a distance will become *more* important than in-person presence.
• Face-to-face meetings are the best form of business communication—even with all their limitations.	• Sometimes other media will be *better* than in-person meetings. Good leaders will choose which medium is the best fit for the task.
• The best leaders are hands-on, in-person leaders—without micromanaging.	• The best leaders will skirt the uncanny valley of eerie over-connection.

FIGURE 21 The new literacy of being there when you are not there, to bridge the uncanny valley and be *better* than being there

The physical world will have a constant virtual overlay. We will all be able to choose what we see and what we don't want to see.

Figure 21 is my summary of the shift toward better than being there.

The literacy of beyond being there will require a range of new skills, including the maker instinct—as it applies to yourself so you can re-make how you lead—and what Silicon Valley visionary Howard Rheingold first called smart-mob organizing, to weave together the distributed organization you are leading.

The literacy of beyond being there will require leaders to apply the maker instinct to themselves.

The Maker Instinct: The ability to turn one's natural instinct to build into a skill for making the future and connecting with others who are making the future. The maker instinct is basic to leadership in the future.

The maker instinct will be needed to re-make yourself and develop your own blended-reality flair.

In 2013, Mike Zuckerman convinced the owner of a three-story building in San Francisco's SOMA district to rent it to him for one month for one dollar. Zuckerman (known affectionately in Silicon Valley as The Other Zuck) created a maker space for artists, makers, builders, and whoever else happened to wander in, and [freespace] was born. It operates under the following principles:

- All our custom code will be open source.
- All our contributions (and those of our community) will be licensed under Creative Commons.
- We will work to document our process so others can learn from us and replicate it in their own communities.
- We will acknowledge and thank those who contribute to the community.
- We welcome participation as long as the safety of our community and participants is not threatened.

The first [freespace] operated for three months and got special attention from the White House on the Civic Day of National Hacking. Now, [freespace] efforts are under way throughout the world, taking various forms. In Greece it's being used to help engage immigrants in creating new worlds for themselves.

[freespace] builds on the maker instinct and applies it to people in need. To create a blended-reality presence, leaders will need to apply the maker instinct to themselves and create new ways to see, nurture, and develop distributed networks. [freespace] is a radical example of that from which we can all learn.

The literacy of beyond being there will require leaders to become smart-mob organizers.

Smart-Mob Organizing: The ability to bring together, engage with, and nurture purposeful business or social-change networks through intelligent use of electronic and other media.

Smart-mob organizing allows you to pull together people to help do what you need to do—using a wide range of media appropriate to the task at hand. Leaders need to find the right people and connect with them at the right time through the best media for the tasks at hand.

Over the last few years, many of our custom forecasts at IFTF have dealt with the future of retail. Certainly, Amazon has changed the retail game, and there is good reason to expect that they will continue to do so. But there are serious alternatives coming to life in Africa. One of the most interesting is the Balogun Market, the biggest open market in Nigeria, which is now accessible via WhatsApp. Individual sellers post new items they have available to their WhatsApp customers, or people can reach out to individual sellers for something specific. Balogunmarket.ng aggregates this behavior into a platform: you reach out to the physical Balogun Market sellers and tell them what you are looking for. They form a WhatsApp group with you and several sellers in the informal market who have that particular product. They send images, and then bargaining begins within the group. At the end, Balogunmarket.ng facilitates payment and delivery. In this way, high-frequency store retailing is formalizing, but not simplifying. This is an example of smart-mob organizing applied to retail.

Another example comes from inside a company. IFTF was asked by the senior executive team at W. L. Gore to do a custom forecast that focused on the next generation of leaders across the firm. This was unusual, since IFTF typically reports its custom forecast to the CEO, the head of innovation, or the head of strategy. Gore is an early adopter in non-hierarchical, network-style leadership. Smart-mob organizing is a way of life at Gore (although most of them don't call it that), since they always want to get as many people involved as possible. IFTF worked with a global team of young leaders to go deep on external future forces likely to disrupt the Gore business—and to draw out implications for the Gore strategy.

As we created the custom forecast, the Gore team set out to create a kind of smart mob within the company—and even with some of its suppliers and partners. They used a very clever application of simple conference calling and screen-sharing media. The three leaders of this global team were in Delaware, Arizona, and Germany, with thirty team members scattered around the world. As IFTF created drafts of the forecast, we distributed drafts in PowerPoint, with a brief voice recording of the forecast. We then did conference-call presentations of the draft for thirty minutes, followed by breakout groups through their own smaller conference calls. Finally, we came back together in a series of iterations until the forecast was finished. It was still an outside-in forecast—not a consensus forecast—but the thirty global team members got a behind-the-scenes view of the custom forecast as it was taking shape. They worked closely with the IFTF team to figure out how best to communicate the forecast to the rest of the company and link it to strategy recommendations. These rising star leaders didn't just communicate the custom forecast to the executive team, they translated it into strategy recommendations.

The young leaders drew from this foresight to propose a new enterprise strategy, which they then presented to the current top leaders. This is a case where the foresight clearly provoked new insights about strategy and fed directly into the strategy process. It also was the first time we worked almost exclusively with next-generation leaders.

Susan Desmond-Hellmann demonstrated smart-mob organizing by engaging more than 2500 people in a massive multiplayer online game. As Chancellor of University of California, San Francisco, she needed the community of faculty and staff to activate their imaginations about the future of education, research, and global health. But she wouldn't be able to convene the whole faculty and staff around a single conference room table, so she chose a blended-reality leadership strategy instead. Using the Institute for the Future's Foresight Engine platform, Hellmann invited the community to imagine the year 2025. The call to action? Play the game, make the future of UCSF. The response? Faculty and staff generated 24,711 ideas in just 36 hours. Through a kind of smart-mob organizing, Hellmann engaged the community to lay the groundwork for some of the strategic decisions of the intervening years. The explosion of ideas was invigorating, but the leadership team had to translate those ideas into strategy and action steps—which they have now done.*

---

* For a more detailed description of this particular example of smart-mob organizing, see http://www.iftf.org/ucsf2025/. For a more general description of the Foresight Engine and how it can be used for massive online multiplayer gaming, see http://www.iftf.org/foresightengine/.

CHAPTER 8

Moving Toward a Future That Is BEYOND Being There

THE GREAT NEWS IS THAT THE BLENDED-REALITY WORLD of leadership in the future will be media rich, with lots of exciting choices for communicating. The challenging news for leaders is that they will have to have experience with how to lead in the expanding array of media-rich worlds and—most importantly—they will have to get very good at deciding which medium is good for what. Richer media mixes, however, may not be better than simpler forms.

> **SURPRISE** The audio channel will be more important than video.

For leadership presence at a distance in a blended-reality world, the audio medium will be a much richer medium than video—and harder to get right.

In my experience, the audio medium has always been undervalued. Video is usually assumed to be richer, more vivid, and sexier. So much energy goes into good video for meetings, so little into good audio. Yet, throughout my career, audio has always been the medium that is most difficult to get right in almost any setup. Without good audio, everything else about communication degrades.

For leaders at a distance, audio will be the primary medium. If your audio channel is weak or scratchy, you will have a weak or scratchy leadership voice—literally and symbolically. Leadership voice will be critical, and audio will be the most important channel to bring your voice to life.

Early in my career, the question of audio vs. video for meetings at a distance was raised in a seminal article whose title I will never forget: "Is Video Valuable or Is Audio Adequate?" The conclusion of this research by the Communications Studies Group in London was that audio only was certainly adequate for most forms of interpersonal communication (Pye 1977). It was difficult to measure additional value that video with audio provided over good audio alone. Certainly, video adds something to audio, and perhaps when people haven't met, good video helps with orientation and trust building. But is video really as important as we tend to think it is? This article argued that it was not, but nobody seems to have listened and they are still not listening.

I believe that future leaders will invest in very high quality audio. Great audio will be a very good investment in leadership presence. I'm not against the video medium and I think it can be useful, but I think it will be far less important for leaders than vivid audio. I believe that the centerpiece of virtual presence will be vivid audio.

Blended-reality media will provide new opportunities to communicate more effectively, productively, and persuasively than ever before. These same vivid media will also create new forms of remote presence that will have the potential to be off-putting, alienating, and even inhuman. This concern was articulated elegantly in 1970 when robotics professor Masahiro Mori at the Tokyo Institute of Technology wrote a classic essay in which he coined the vivid term *uncanny valley* to describe how humans react to humanoid robots: "I have noticed that, in climbing toward the goal of making robots appear human, our affinity for them increases until we come to a valley ... which I call the *uncanny valley*" (Mori 2012).

I expect that a new kind of uncanny valley will appear on the horizon as the media for leadership at a distance become increasingly powerful,

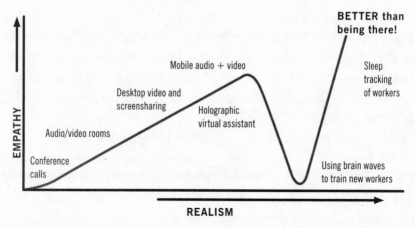

FIGURE 22 The Uncanny Valley for Distributed-Leadership Organizations

as blended-reality leadership comes to include both human and artificial intelligence. Paraphrasing Professor Mori, in climbing toward the goal of leaders being there without being there, our affinity for those leaders will increase until we reach an uncanny valley where leaders will be perceived as being weirdly present. Building on the original uncanny valley graphic that plots the relationship between empathy and increasing realism, I suggest an uncanny valley for distributed leadership that will look something like Figure 22.

High-quality audio is great for creating a sense of presence at a distance, as is video. Our tools for room and desktop audio and video are getting better. On the good side of the uncanny valley, there are many options for audio, video, and mixed media communications.

Dropping into the uncanny valley are some of the emerging array of holographic virtual assistants. They must strike a delicate balance between realism and spookiness. Research on using brain waves of successful employees to model and train new employees seems deep in the uncanny valley to me. Sleep tracking could be similarly eerie if a leader is tracking the sleep of people working on his team. Would you want your boss to know automatically if you didn't sleep well the night before?

The challenge for the future of distributed leadership is we don't yet know what could be on the other side of the uncanny valley for leadership at a distance. I doubt that it is a leadership experience that will be the *same as if* the leader were there in person. Rather, it will need to be a hybrid of human presence and machine support. And it will need to be better than if the leader were there in person.

In the transitional period, which has already begun, leaders will be present in a variety of ways much more of the time. Ambient presence could be reassuring if there is trust in the leader, but threatening or spooky, if not. Leaders will be able to monitor performance with much greater detail, even if they are not physically present. What used to be called *workflow systems* earlier in my career will be capable of much more detailed monitoring of progress—or lack of progress—through a ubiquitous mesh of sensors. On one side, some could perceive blended-reality presence as Big Brother incarnate, with performance monitoring turning into eavesdropping, measuring stress levels and emotional states, and cataloging worker output on a minute-by-minute basis. Such tracking might even help leaders in the short term, but such behavior would cross into the uncanny valley of inhumane co-presence that is unwanted, uninvited, and difficult to shake.

On the other side of this leadership uncanny valley lies the promised land of leadership at a distance, a presence that will be better than in person. And though technology will have an important role in enabling this kind of presence, the best examples of it I have seen involve no technology at all.

These are the human resources issues of the future. Will those handling human resources be ready for this shift? So many of today's HR departments have been degraded, downsized, and even outsourced. For those who are in these roles, my advice is to avoid the term *HR* and instead call yourselves Human . . . Resources, with a pause for emphasis. Human resources will be so important in this future, to avoid the uncanny valley and bridge into new media and styles of leadership that thrives by being there without being there.

As we move into a world of ambient communications media, many will fall into the uncanny valley of leadership at a distance. In climbing toward the goal of leaders being there without being there, our affinity for those leaders will increase as their virtual connection increases—until they reach an uncanny valley where leaders are perceived as being weirdly or inappropriately present. Do we really want our leaders to appear virtually as if they were there in person, or can we do better, and at the same time avoid the uncanny valley?

I have worked with several companies over the years where founders had such strong leadership presence that it was as if they were there with us in the room. When I did a project with Disney, for example, people on the team referred to Walt as if he were there with us. They seemed to know with confidence what Walt would say if we asked him for advice. In some sense, he really was there with us, and his presence didn't seem weird to me. In fact, it was kind of comforting and useful. I suspect that my emotional comfort was a function of the Disney folks I had in the room with me, who were bringing their living voices to the founder's ideas. Clearly, however, my experience of Walt's presence could seem uncanny to some people.

Similarly, at W. L. Gore & Associates, founder Bill Gore was such a charismatic presence that he continues to live throughout the company. His eloquent quotes are on the walls, and his presence is baked into the culture. Bill Gore was an outdoors guy, and Gore offices play to the needs of outdoor people. At most meetings that I have attended at Gore, someone referred to Bill at least once. Again, it was as if he were there with us, even though he is no longer living. His presence is an essential part of their culture. Many of the leaders there today seem to embody Bill Gore's values and priorities across the generations. Again, however, this kind of founder presence could become uncanny and unproductive for some.

At Walmart, it is as if Sam Walton is still alive. His office paneling and furnishings were moved to a downtown Bentonville museum when he died. The current CEO Doug McMillon works in an exact replica of Sam Walton's office now. Sam Walton's truck is still intact at the museum. His values are written on the walls and in the minds of people who work at Walmart. His family still controls the board, so his values live on.

If magnetic leaders, with clear and consistent values and vision, can project a presence even when they are no longer alive, how might living leaders feel and be present while lacking only physical proximity?

In-person conversation skills will still be very important, but in-person meetings will happen in the context of a blended-reality world. We can't go back to the way it was. We need to go forward to a mixed-media world that also includes the conversation skills we'll need in the new blended reality we are creating.

Of course to begin with, a leader needs a vivid presence that is strong and worth sharing. But given that, the next decade presents new opportunities for communicating whatever leadership presence you have as effectively as possible over long distances. The best leaders will figure out how to be there without being there.

Shared Presence

This will be a world where co-presence is possible, even when people are not present physically together at the same place and same time. Mixed-reality experiences will be able to be shared across distances. The best leaders will have vivid shared work and life experiences with the people they lead. Physically distant leaders will want to feel close—but not *too* close.

This will be a world where sensors are ubiquitous, many of them are connected, and some of them will be in our bodies. Moreover, leaders (and everyone else) will have the ability to make sense out of all that sensor data. These embodied systems will be able to link workers with leaders through biomarkers.

The best leaders will be able to literally embody and sense the mood of the people they are leading without intruding on their privacy.

This will be a world where we can finally put to rest the old notion that the only productive workers are those who are physically present and able to be seen by their leaders. The adage "Arrive at the office before your boss; leave after him" will make little sense in this world because the outcomes of work will become much more explicit and measurable. The traditional "8 to 5" jobs will yield to ways of making a living that are focused on outcomes—not physical presence (unless that is required for a particular work outcome). Certainly telework in simple formats already happen today, but the future will be far more complex and robust.

Tracking progress will become much easier, but the tools used to do so will raise the key questions of what should be tracked and what constitutes progress. The potential for worker abuse will rise, as systems will have the ability to measure almost everything, and sometimes they will measure the wrong things.

Leaders will need to develop their own sophistication in the art and science of being there without being there. There are some general directions of change. For instance, leaders will have to shift from thinking about physical proximity to attentional proximity and come to see scheduling as a much more dynamic and ad hoc process. But, on the whole, communications strategies will have to become much more situational.

In May of 2016, Institute for the Future's Tech Lab Program created a new ten-year forecast of the disruptive shift from technology tools to media ecology. Called "When Everything Is Media," this forecast identified the media that will be available to leaders thinking ten years ahead. This chapter draws heavily from that research.

I believe that this shift from technology to media began in about 2010, as I described in Chapter 2 on the future of looking long. The shift from separate technology tools to media created new abilities to look long with precision and perspective. New media for leadership were a piece of this new world that began to open up in 2010. Now, the possibilities are becoming much clearer as the young people who became adults in 2010 are beginning to join the workforce. They will be bringing new media skills with them—often from the world of video gaming—and enter the workforce armed with technological sophistication and connectivity. In 2010, the user interfaces and power of video gaming was roughly ten times better than typical office systems. Now, the gap has narrowed. The office is catching up with the video gamers. This mix of technology capabilities and skills in media use will fuel dramatic shifts.

Looking out to 2027, dramatically improved technological capacities will create a new media context for leadership. In each of these zones, new capabilities are emerging. Soon, some of these new capabilities will be ubiquitous. They will be the basic tools of leadership. Each leader will need to become very skilled at choosing which medium is good for what and how to communicate their own personal style of leadership—with flair—through the chosen media. There will be more choices and better choices than those we have now, but it will require leaders to be creative to develop their own presence and flair.

The potential for corporations without people, as I introduced in Chapter 6 on the future of distributed organizations, will raise new issues of how to lead distributed organizations. The best leaders will figure out ways to track and guide the progress of work without prying or preying.

The Miku Story

Consider a radical future where distributed leaders could literally embody the people they lead. Hatsune Miku is a Japanese pop star whose name roughly translates as "the first sound from the future." (See Figure 23.)

Miku is not a human, but many humans contribute to her being. She gives live concerts as a singing, dancing holographic image to sold-out crowds. The crowds are live, even though Miku is not. Miku's holographic rendering sings and dances with live musicians; she has even performed an opera with a human orchestra.

Miku is described on the website of her creator Crypton Future Media as the "beloved collaboratively constructed cyber celebrity with a growing user community across the world." Creative Commons licensing has allowed this virtual pop star to have more than 100,000 songs written for her and 1,000,000 created artworks.

The online crowd choreographs her dance steps. Contributors use what has come to be called *vocaloid* software to create her voice and her songs. Her fans treat her like a real singer, except that it is those same fans that create her music and her dancing. Without her fans, Miku would be nothing. They write songs from her point of view, as if she were a real person singing about her life. Other fans take her songs and create artwork and videos of Miku singing and dancing.

I believe that Miku is an early signal for a new kind of distributed leadership and worker engagement that will become possible over the next decade.

Linh K. Le is a double major in anthropology and political science at the University of California, Irvine, who is pursuing a career as a diplomat. I think, given his interests, that he is showing great foresight by studying Miku. He recently published a fascinating analysis of Miku, in which he points out that, in most cases to date, events in real life have inspired innova-

「初音ミク」公式イラストレーター
KEI氏による完全描きおこし！

幸せな未来が永遠に続くことを願い、描きおこされたオリジナルイラスト。
ウェディング姿に身を包んだ「初音ミク」が
おふたりの末永い幸せをお祈りいたします。

LOVING BRIDE BLUE LOVING BRIDE PINK

ウェディングドレスのイメージに
ピッタリなブルーの婚姻届が登場！
可愛いドレスで着飾ったミクが
キュートな雰囲気のデザイン。

あたたかな家庭を築いてゆくおふたりに
ピッタリなピンクの婚姻届が登場！
大輪の花が舞う中、たたずむミクが
上品な雰囲気のデザイン。

FIGURE 23 Anime pop star Hatsune Miku performs for live audiences.

tion in social media. Miku is different: she was created through social media and is now inspiring innovation in real life (Le 2013). I think she will inspire new models for leadership in shape-shifting organizations. In a distributed autonomous organization (DAO) such as I described earlier, could it be possible to have a Miku-style CEO? Oh my.

But seriously, imagine a human CEO who has a Miku-style advisor, an intelligent agent (perhaps with an avatar) that embodies the current views of the people who work for the CEO, as well as, perhaps, the company's customers. The advisor would embody all the key constituencies and, through big data analytics, provide a much more accurate sense of how workers and customers perceive the company, its marketplace, and its choices. Imagine the distributed leadership model inspired by Miku in Figure 24.

When technology disrupts, it often reveals human strengths and weaknesses. Miku, through her vocaloid software to create her music and 3-D animation software to choreograph her dance routines, is able to crowdsource collaboration in ways that humans could not do alone without digital assistance and connection.

The foresight is that a Miku-style CEO advisor could be an advocate for the community of workers. A Miku-style CEO advisor could also be

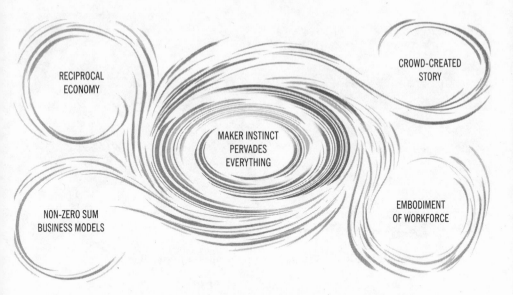

RECIPROCAL ECONOMY

CROWD-CREATED STORY

MAKER INSTINCT PERVADES EVERYTHING

NON-ZERO SUM BUSINESS MODELS

EMBODIMENT OF WORKFORCE

FIGURE 24 The distributed leadership model inspired by Miku: human/avatar symbiosis combines strengths and weaknesses of humans and machines

an informant in the best sense of the word, to communicate difficult topics to the CEO without violating individual privacy. Each human leader could design or choose his or her own Miku-style advisor to emphasize what they feel is most important. The Miku-style advisor (an intelligent agent) would embody and express the will of workers and the customers.

The insight is that a human CEO would still embody the values of the firm. If crowd-sourcing software could do a better job of tapping into worker attitudes, issues, and concerns, human leaders would have more time to do what they do best.

Figure 25 illustrates the process that leaders will need to follow to lead in ways that are beyond being there.

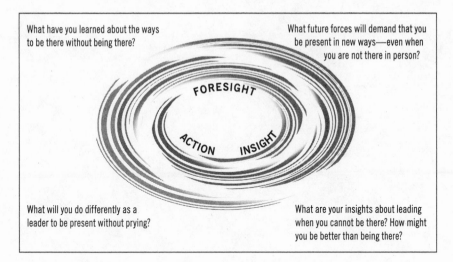

What have you learned about the ways to be there without being there?

What future forces will demand that you be present in new ways—even when you are not there in person?

FORESIGHT

ACTION   INSIGHT

What will you do differently as a leader to be present without prying?

What are your insights about leading when you cannot be there? How might you be better than being there?

FIGURE 25 The new literacy of being there when you are not there, to bridge the uncanny valley and be *better* than being there

CHAPTER 9

The *New Literacy* of Creating and Sustaining Positive Energy

THOSE WHO ARE FLUENT IN THE NEW LITERACY OF creating and sustaining positive energy will say:

- When I walk into a room, I radiate positive energy.
- I have a disciplined approach to my own physical, mental, and spiritual (not necessarily religious) fitness in the face of my daily work pressures, my private life, and the external world.
- I balance my personal energy throughout my working day (I moderate my peaks and droops), and I am resilient under pressure.
- I create space for the people I lead to balance their own physical, mental, and spiritual energy.

I did a talk recently for a group of CIOs in Silicon Valley. As I talked about the need for leaders to bring positive energy to work, one of the CIOs interrupted me and said: "Ah, you know about the chi suckers!"

This CIO was of Chinese descent, and he was using the term *chi* to refer to the energy force of an individual. This CIO—who radiated positive energy—was a chi booster, but he was sometimes in rooms with chi suckers. Indeed, some people seem to suck the energy out of a room.

Bob Sutton from Stanford taught me many years ago that, based on his extensive research on innovation, the easiest way for people to look smart in a meeting is to be negative. Those who bring negative energy to work, however, drag all of us down.

> As the research shows, the more time you spend around rotten apples— those lousy, lazy, grumpy, and nasty people—the more damage you will suffer. When people are emotionally depleted, they stop focusing on their jobs and instead work on improving their moods. If you find that there are a few subordinates who are so unpleasant that, day after day, they sap the energy you need to inspire others and feel good about your own job, my advice—if you can't get rid of them—is to spend as little time around them as possible. (Sutton 2010)

Rick Karp, the leader of Cole Hardware in San Francisco (one of the most innovative hardware stores in the world and the first hardware store on the internet), refers to "toxic personalities" who consistently lower the energy levels of people they are around. I'm confident that we've all experienced toxic personalities, or at least toxic behavior. Perhaps these negative role models can at least inspire us to imagine the opposite: a positive life force that brings personal energy to his or her leadership, one you can feel when that person walks in the room.

I have trouble specifying exactly what constitutes positive energy in leaders, but I certainly know it when I see it. When I do leadership workshops, I sometimes ask groups to stand and close their eyes. Then, I ask them to imagine themselves coming into a room with people they have never met before. I ask them to express positive energy with their bodies, to exude and radiate positive energy without saying anything.

Almost everyone smiles to express positive energy, but they are not booming smiles. Some open their palms and face them up. Many people focus on their posture, to stand up straight and keep centered. Some open their arms. Some take a centered position, as practiced in the martial arts. A few strike the Wonder Woman pose: hands on hips, feet wide apart, straight back, strong look forward. Body language is an important way to express positive energy, but there are many different ways.

Mindfulness has become a popular topic and practice in corporate America over the last few years. These practices, while often a bit superficial in my experience, show that interest is there for the kind of new emphasis on fitness that I am forecasting for leaders over the next decade.

Certainly, there are many ways to express positive energy, and each of us has to express our own energy in a way that is authentic for us. I suggest that you watch other leaders and ask how—if at all—they express positive energy. How do they make you feel, beyond what they say? It brings to mind something Maya Angelou said: "I've learned that people will forget what you said, people will forget what you did, but people will never forget how you made them feel."

In 2010, I worked with Humana and Gallup on the topic of well-being, beyond just sick care. Gallup was just beginning its remarkable work on global well-being (Rath and Harter 2010), and Institute for the Future was focused on the future of what we started to call the *global well-being economy*. The last big economic driver was engineering and the digital economy. The next big economic driver will be biology, the life sciences, and the global well-being economy. Engineering will still be important, but it will be bioengineering.

Building on that work and the work I've done since then, I've become convinced that well-being for leaders will involve so much more than not being sick.

If leaders are going to thrive in a future of extreme disruption, they must not only manage their own energy, they must encourage, model, and reward positive energy in others. The tools for energy management are so much better now than they ever were—and they will get ever better over the next decade. Leaders have no excuse now. Fitness will be a price of entry for top leadership roles. Extreme fitness—physical, mental, and even spiritual (though not necessarily religious)—will be required for most leadership roles.

Figure 26 depicts the elements of well-being that I believe will be most important in the future.

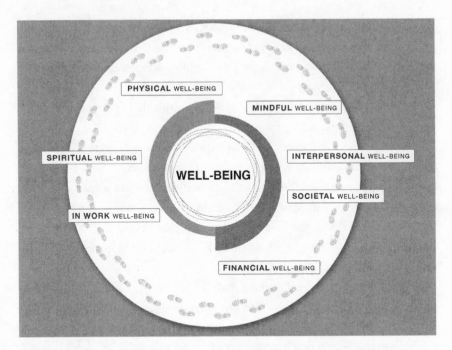

FIGURE 26 The most important elements of well-being for the future

Physical Well-Being: While there is much debate of almost every healthy living practice, everyone seems to agree on the importance of exercise. Here is what former chief medical officer of Google Kelly Traver says: "Exercise physically changes your brain. It helps you learn and remember better. It promotes alertness and enhances creative thinking. It elevates mood and lowers stress. In short, exercise is your biggest ally in achieving and maintaining good health" (Traver & Sargent 2011). When I was president of Institute for the Future, I worked with an excellent executive coach named Pierre Mornell, who reminded me again and again: "More stress, more exercise."

Mindful Well-Being: The good news is neuroscience will get very practical over the next decade. Leaders will have a wide range of new resources to help them develop brain-smart ways of leading. Mindful well-being includes the popular interest in mindfulness, but it emphasizes applying the principles of neuroscience to leadership and daily living.

Interpersonal Well-Being: By interpersonal, I mean family, friends, neighbors, and those with whom you have direct communications on a frequent basis. In order to experience interpersonal well-being you must have a community of individuals with whom you are so close that you could call them at 3 a.m. when you are crying. (Vogel 2016)

Societal Well-Being: This refers to how well linked are you to the culture, the society, and the planet around you.

Financial Well-Being: Consider the idea of "making a living." For many people, making a living means having a job. In the future, however, there will be fewer traditional jobs and lower job security for those who do have them. On the other hand, the new ways of working will allow much greater flexibility and many more ways to make a living. Dee Hock, the founder and former CEO of Visa, summarized this logic well: "Money motivates neither the best people nor the best in people. It can move the body and influence the mind, but it cannot touch the heart or move the spirit" (Hock 199).

In-Work Well-Being: When I was in divinity school, I learned about the intriguing notion of a "calling." A calling is a strong urge, a push even, in a particular vocational direction. In a religious context, a calling often comes from God or a representative of God. I don't believe that is always the case, but certainly a career calling is much more than a casual choice of what you want to do with your life. Leaders, particularly in a work-oriented country like the United States, are at their best if they truly believe in what they are doing at work.

Spiritual Well-Being: Spiritual does not necessarily mean participation in any organized religion. While I am a student of world religions, I am not an

---

* I'm certainly not an expert at making money, but I know it is important—and it will be important—for leaders to have at least a base level of financial compensation. While money will not be the most important motivator for most leaders, it will be important at some level that will vary from leader to leader. Beyond a basic level of financial compensation that makes a leader feel well rewarded and comfortable, financial compensation doesn't seem to matter that much. A recent literature review by the *Harvard Business Review* makes this point well: "Intuitively, one would think that higher pay should produce better results, but scientific evidence indicates that the link between compensation, motivation and performance is much more complex. In fact, research suggests that even if we let people decide how much they should earn, they would probably not enjoy their job more" (Chamorro-Premuzic 2013).

advocate of any particular brand of religion. Religions can provide a sense of meaning for leaders, but there are many different approaches. The key is a sense of grounding, a sense of meaning that allows a leader to maintain a center in spite of being encircled by disruption. Meaning will be illusive in the VUCA world, but there will be a wide range of options for leaders to develop a sense of spiritual well-being—some personally uplifting, some socially constructive, and some downright dangerous.

Over the next decade, a wide range of strategies for leadership well-being will emerge. Here are four examples that I find particularly intriguing—each with its own emphasis. I'm from the Midwest, but I've lived on the East Coast and the West Coast of the United States, and I've traveled to many parts of the world. I've used my personal experience to characterize each approach, although I apologize in advance for a bit of geographic and cultural stereotyping that I intend in a playful way.

An East Coast Strategy for Leadership Well-Being

To create positive energy, you have to have energy within yourself. Balancing your personal energy throughout the day may be the biggest challenge in leadership. Leaders need to literally embody positive energy in consistent ways without wild swings. In many leadership roles, leaders need to be both sprinters and long-distance runners, depending on what is called for in a particular situation. The Corporate Athlete is the best-known program for *personal energy management*, the term they use to describe the kind of holistic fitness that is necessary for high performance in business. It was created in 1992 by performance psychologist Dr. Jim Loehr and exercise physiologist Jack Groppel and is now part of the High Performance Institute at Johnson & Johnson.

Rituals are necessary at each stage to keep the practices alive and growing. We all need our own rituals, rituals that have meaning for us, rituals that we will continue doing every day. But each of us will be motivated differently. Our personal rituals will need to be consistent with our own personal motivations for fitness.

The Corporate Athlete is focused on balancing your physical needs with what you're trying to achieve in business. It provides you with different ways to think about and improve your own fitness in a way that makes you both healthier and more productive. The Corporate Athlete program includes strong guidance about exercise, nutrition, and mental balance. In particular, it emphasizes the need for resiliency that is often much more difficult for executives to maintain than for competitive athletes, whose training regimen tends to be seasonal or of limited duration.

Well-being programs akin to the Corporate Athlete are scaling the idea of energy balancing for corporate leaders. A range of other options is also appearing, and often they are being built into corporate benefit packages. The challenge as these programs scale is to have lasting impacts on how leaders work and live. The danger will be that a great program like Corporate Athlete gets watered down into an insurance company newsletter on health living. I think of the Corporate Athlete as an "East Coast" approach to leadership fitness. It is highly structured and can be competitive, with a focus on immersion experiences. For many people, it is both life changing and wonderful.

A West Coast Strategy for Leadership Well-Being

Stanford-trained internal medicine physician Kelly Traver developed what I think of as a "West Coast" approach and tested it while she was chief medical officer at Google. The program now has a telemedicine component and is branded as Healthiest You. It was bought by and is now available through Teladoc as of 2016.* The subtitle of her book, *Healthiest You*, which is based on this approach, expresses her basic belief in the importance of neuroscience for motivation: *Take Charge of Your Brain to Take Charge of Your Life* (Traver 2011).

Kelly Traver has created a brain-based guide to help people understand their own personal top motivators. Most of us are affected by all of them to some degree, but Traver argues that the majority of people are strongly influenced by just a few. Keeping in mind what motivates you individually

* Whether or not these particular examples are commercially successful, I am forecasting that a range of similar services will become available. http://www.healthiestyou.com/#/.

can guide the kind of healthy living program that will make the most sense for you. Which of these motivators are most important for you to consider as you design your own program for physical, mental, and spiritual fitness? To me, this seems to boil down to what you are passionate about.

Competition: These people do best when challenged and when they can compete explicitly with others. The closer the competition, the better, for some.

Self-Mastery: People who are motivated by self-mastery enjoy doing a good job simply for its own sake. They do well by achieving small successes that build on one another.

Social Connection: These people are motivated best when working on health goals together with others.

Tangible Rewards: Some do best when aiming for clear outcomes that have associated rewards.

Curiosity: People motivated by curiosity will do best when learning more about whatever it is they are working on. Information is power and motivation to these people. For example, if an individual is working on stress management, he or she will do much better by learning how and why stress has the mental and physical effects it does rather than simply being told to meditate.

Purpose: Those who are motivated by being part of something bigger could consider training for a race that raises funds for cancer research.

Playfulness: People who are motivated by playfulness do well making a game out of exercise/fitness.

Helping Others: People who like to help others can be motivated, for example, when they understand how their personal health and wellness needs affect others.

Recognition: These are people who like to achieve, but do best when someone else recognizes and rewards them for their achievements.

Structure: These people do best with a concrete schedule and plan. They thrive when able to plan and predict their own world. (Traver 2011, 38–40)

Dr. Traver argues that you should not just go into a fitness program; you should first figure out what motivates your brain. Once you know that, then you design your fitness program so it matches your neuro patterns and the things that tend to motivate you.

Nutrition is particularly important for physical and mental fitness, and this is the best summary I've seen about how to approach what and how we eat.

> The best way to eat to provide for maximum energy is to have four or five small, frequent meals per day so that the body and brain have constant access to glucose (sugar). The trick here is to take in small amounts so your body doesn't have more than it needs; otherwise it will convert the excess calories into fat. The other trick is to consume foods with high fiber, complex carbohydrates that contain some protein and perhaps a little unsaturated fat but are not high in simple carbohydrates (sugar) or refined carbohydrates (for instance, white bread and rice), because that will give you a rapid blood sugar spike that will leave you hungry and exhausted after about two hours. (Traver 2011, 126)

A Global Strategy for Leadership Well-Being

National Geographic funded a project to find the places on earth where people live the longest, happiest lives. The Blue Zones Project focused on the ideal cycle of life: live long, live healthy, but die quickly. The key variables all linked back to interpersonal well-being. Journalist Dan Buettner has written extensively about it, and there is now an active movement to create Blue Zone cities and regions (Buettner 2010). When the original research was done in 2003, only one of these special places was in the United States: a Seventh Day Adventist community outside of Los Angeles. If you look across all those regions of the world, the principles that seem to lead to long and happy lives emphasize the importance of interpersonal relationships to maintain health and energy balance.

The Blue Zone Project uses the term *plant slant*. Plant-focused diets are clearly a wave of the future, for many reasons.

Also, consider the 80-percent rule that is used in Okinawa, Japan: we should all stop eating when we are 80-percent full. That's a basic discipline of life that goes back to Confucius. For me, this rule of thumb is so simple, but so difficult to practice (Buettner 2008).

Most of the cities in the Blue Zones are not healthiest because residents are going to the gym and doing intense exercise programs. Rather, it's mostly due to walking. People there are getting out and moving naturally. The healthiest of these areas have hills that people walk up and down. It's built into their way of living. Many of these natural movements are done together with people who stay close for years and years. In Blue Zones, continuity in relationships is critical to long-term healthy living, and having real purpose is important to long life and happiness. Downshifting is similar to what many companies call mindfulness training now.

An Integrative Strategy for Leadership Well-Being

Integrative medicine methods are getting so much better now that leaders have resources they never had before. For example, Dr. Brad Jacobs is the founder of BlueWave Medicine. He has developed what he calls the 6 Pillars of Healthy Living (see Figure 27).

I especially like the names of these healthy living practices; they are

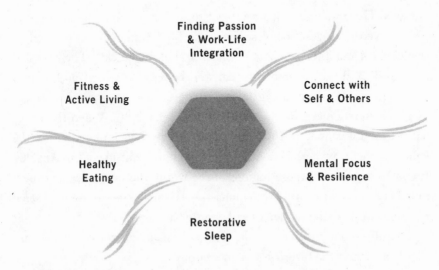

FIGURE 27 An integrative strategy for leadership well-being.
Courtesy of BlueWave Medicine

simple but powerful. They all flow into each other, and each has a direct or indirect impact on health. They are organized into a simple self-assessment that is intended to start a conversation about health and well-being. It is recommended that you start with the area that you are most excited about and enjoy the most. Here is a taste of the BlueWave self-assessment, each item on a five-point scale.*

- I know a lot about how food impacts my overall health.
- I don't have any health problems that are attributed to a lack of physical activity.
- I get 7–8 hours of sleep most nights.
- I have breaks scheduled into my day specifically for the purpose of renewal/recharging my brain and body.
- I make time to take care of myself emotionally and to align myself with my personal life goals as much as I'd like.
- If I were to die today, I would die feeling that, for the most part, I had lived the life I wanted.

This integrative approach seeks to combine the best of conventional medicine with alternative and lifestyle medicine practices. The practice includes concierge primary care, acupuncture, bodywork, massage, psychotherapy, yoga, personal training, and health coaching. BlueWave is grounded in the following definition of integrative medicine and health: "the practice of medicine that reaffirms the importance of the relationship between the practitioner and the patient, focuses on the whole person, is informed by evidence, and makes use of all appropriate therapeutic approaches, health care professionals, and disciplines to achieve optimal health and healing."**

---

* http://www.drbradjacobs.com/meet-dr-brad/6-key-pillars-healthy-living. Dr. Jacobs is Chair of the Academy of Integrative Health and Medicine (www.aihm.org). The Academy recognizes the similar processes unfolding in the field of health that I am discussing in this world. The Academy is about bringing a virtual and in-person community together of all health professionals through on-line and in-person Inter-professional education, dialogue, membership, and community.

** https://www.imconsortium.org/about/about-us.cfm.

Current Literacy	Future Literacy
• Healthy = not sick; leaders don't think much about well-being.	• Leaders will body-hack for super well-being.
• Neuroscience is not a topic leaders think much about or benefit from.	• Neuroscience will be practical for savvy leaders.
• Leaders perform best at the center of their competence.	• Leaders will perform best at the edge of their competence.
• Workers often struggle to find hope.	• Leaders will be very good at seeding hope for others.

FIGURE 28 The new literacy of creating and sustaining positive energy

There is no magic in any approach. The important thing for leaders is to develop their own programs based on what motivates them, and then stick to it. I believe that any of the strategies outlined above will help leaders to create and sustain positive energy in their leadership. Every leader will need to find or create a good approach that works for them. If you're going to be a successful leader in the disruptive world of the future, you will need to be extremely fit and project positive energy in your leadership.

Is it possible for a leader to radiate too much energy? Yes.

Figure 28 provides a summary of the shift that will play out over the next ten years in terms of creating personal energy.

Creating positive energy will require many skills, especially bio-empathy and quiet transparency.

The literacy of creating and sustaining positive energy will require nurturing bio-empathy with yourself.

Bio-Empathy: The ability to see things from nature's point of view; to understand, respect, and learn from nature's patterns. Nature has its own clarity, if only we humans can understand and learn from it.

Bio-empathy involves learning the principles of nature and applying them to yourself in order to develop your own body and mind—as well as your own leadership style. We all need bio-empathy, but we especially need bio-empathy with our own bodies and with our own brain centers.

An important part of bio-empathy with yourself is what is usually referred to as work-life balance. Ellen Galinsky, the founder of the Families and Work Institute in New York City, has done the deepest research on the intersections between life at work and life at home. She concluded years ago that work–life "balance" is extremely difficult in today's world, and I believe that will be even more true in the future. Instead, Ellen Galinsky recommends that we pursue work-life "navigation." As with any other form of navigation, there are some fixed "rocks" that must be avoided, but there are also many "currents" that are more fluid. Most importantly, there are lots of choices. All of us who work also have personal lives; we all have some relationships outside of work. Work–life "integration" is also a term that is becoming popular, but some people really do want separation of their work and private life, not integration.

While I wonder if work-life balance is even possible, I am intrigued by the concept of work-life navigation. In a blended-reality world there has to be a blend of work and private life; you just can't separate them. Achieving balance may be unrealistic, but you can navigate artfully. Human resource organizations can give people choices and help them navigate.

The literacy of creating and sustaining positive energy will require quiet transparency with strength, humility, and empathy.

Quiet Transparency: The ability to be open and transparent about what matters to you, without advertising yourself.

I believe that the age of the rock star leaders is over. We will still have rock star leaders, but they won't tend to last long. Certainly, a few will survive, but wannabe rock star leaders will become easy targets in social media, even if unfairly.

We all have to be centered enough that we have a sense of strength combined with a sense of humility. After the Golden State Warriors lost Game 3 of the NBA Finals to Cleveland in 2016, their coach Steve Kerr said this about his star guard Stephen Curry: "Humility with an arrogance. It's an awesome thing" (Jenkins 2016).

I was on a program with Alan Mulally, who at the time was CEO of Ford Motor Company. He embodied quiet transparency: he was strong, humble, and empathetic. We were both presenting to a room full of senior executives from a variety of industries who had been gathered by the Gartner Group. Alan came in early and sat in the back of the room to get a sense of the group. When he was introduced, he went table to table shaking hands with people before he went up front. Compare that to how most CEOs or keynote speakers enter a room. Often, they arrive late or just in time, and they come directly to the front of the room; then, they leave with very little personal contact. Alan Mulally was personally engaging for everyone in that room.

He talked about the pressures when he came in as CEO of Ford in a time of crisis. One of his basic strategies in the One Ford campaign was what he called "accountability through transparency." He set up weekly business plan reviews, but he opened these meetings to everyone. The pressure to present when anyone could be present was its own accountability, he argued, and much more effective than typical top-down methods. These weekly reviews "would shine a light onto the darkest corners of the company. . . . In a company like Ford, the weak went to the wall; only the strong survived. Now they were being told they were all on the same team, and Mulally expected them to act like it" (Hoffman 2013).

In 2016, I was the keynote speaker for the 250 top nurses and nursing executives at Northwell Health, the largest health care provider in the state of New York. I had never done a talk to a large group of nurses before, and I wasn't sure how it would go. I came away so impressed with the role of nurses; they may in fact be the best prepared to thrive in the VUCA world. The best nurses embody quiet transparency: strength, humility, and empathy. They are trained in the principles of nature, and they understand what it takes to create positive energy. Also, most hospitals and health care institutions have a shape-shifting quality—even if it does hang over what are often painfully bureaucratic structures. And health care is perhaps the most advanced industry in using immersive learning methods. The Northwell nurses were inspiring for me.

CHAPTER 10

Moving Toward a Future Where Leaders Are Body Hackers

WHILE MANY LEADERS IN THE PAST HAD UNHEALTHY lifestyles, that will not be an option in the future because of the intense pressure of leading in a world of extreme disruption and distributed everything. Almost all successful leaders will be physically, mentally, and spiritually strong. By spiritual, I don't necessarily mean religious, but grounded with a sense of meaning in the face of the VUCA world.

SURPRISE   The best leaders will be super-fit.

Over the next decade, sensors will be everywhere and neuroscience will get practical. And if they pay attention with personal rigor and grit, leaders will benefit dramatically. Using body hacking, leaders will be able to monitor and enhance their own energy levels, as well as engage with people who work with them through body sensitivities and metrics.

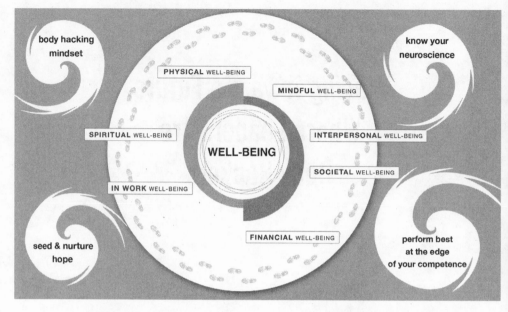

FIGURE 29 Positive energy creation resulting from various states of well-being

In Figure 29, you can see how the future of positive energy creation will be characterized by leaders who

- use body hacking to enhance their own performance—and the performance of other workers
- use neuroscience principles in practical ways
- perform best when they are at the edge of their own competence
- seed hope in the face of the VUCA world

Body Hacking for High Performance

I use the term *hacking* in a positive way, but I'm from Silicon Valley. In Silicon Valley, hacking is creating, growing, making, or remaking—unless it happens to be illegal. We have hackathons of many kinds on a daily basis here. In other parts of the world, any activity described as hacking may be perceived as illegal or at least legally suspect.

To me, hacking means to start from something as it is, but make it better in a way that is not illegal. My IFTF colleague Daria Lamb thinks of hacking as chipping away at borders and barriers to the value that is trapped within. I like that.

In the future, we will all have tremendous ability to hack our own bodies, to zoom in and zoom out with high-resolution views, in a way that only a few people can today. High-resolution body hacking will allow leaders to make and remake their own bodies, enhance personal energy levels and performance, and help them be more prepared for the leadership challenges they will face.

This ability has staggering implications for understanding what contributes to our own health, energy, and well-being.

Ten years from now, how might we hack our physical, mental, and spiritual health in positive ways?

At Institute for the Future, we first used the term *body hacking* in a custom forecast for an East Coast company about fifteen years ago. Our goal was to be provocative, without turning people off. In our forecast language, we want to use terms that are familiar enough to grasp—but that do not sound like the same old thing. *Body hacking*, we found, made some people cringe, and it stopped the conversation. On the other hand, for many people, it started great conversations.

If you want to be a leader in the VUCA world of the future, I believe you will need to be extremely healthy, not just routinely healthy. There will always be different approaches to health and well-being, but if you're going to thrive in a disruptive world, you're going to have to make good choices.

In Chapters 7 and 8 (about being there when you're not there), I explained the risks of the uncanny valley, where leaders will be able to develop very close relationships with workers over large distances but run the risk of being perceived as *too* close. Imagine a world with cheap sensors everywhere, many of which are connected and some of which are in our bodies. It is one thing for a leader to hack his own body to improve his own performance, but what if a leader gets caught in the uncanny valley and gets too close in a way that workers find prying or just weird? Body hacking will make it much easier to get close, but also to get too close.

Body hacking will make some people cringe if their leaders are doing it to themselves, but it might be much more repulsive if leaders try to hack the bodies of their workers. Will there be ways that body hacking can be done in humane and productive ways—without violating privacy or security? We don't know yet, but I suspect that there are—if we can avoid the uncanny valley.

Neuroscience-Savvy Leadership Practices

David Rock is the founder of the NeuroLeadership Institute in New York, the first research group to integrate neuroscience and leadership principles. They are studying things like job performance. They argue that many of the classic performance review systems trigger the fight-or-flight mechanism in our brain and have exactly the opposite effect from what they're supposed to do. They draw upon neuroscience research and apply it to a work environment.

David Rock's book *Your Brain at Work* is a practical handbook for applying neuroscience lessons to specific daily work activities. Using detailed scenarios from days in the life of a young working couple, he applies the research in a practical way.

> I noticed a surprising pattern while putting this book together. I saw that there are five domains of social experience that your brain treats the same as survival issues. These domains form a model, which I call the SCARF model, which stands for Status, Certainty, Autonomy, Relatedness, and Fairness. The model describes the interpersonal primary rewards or threats that are important to the brain. (Rock 2009)

The SCARF model suggests that, in order to be balanced and productive, our brains need to feel a sense of status, some certainty that provides grounding, a sense of autonomy that gives self strength, balanced with a sense of relatedness to others, and finally a sense of fairness in the system. Without these brain balance basics, we feel sapped of energy.

There's a project at Stanford called the Forgiveness Project—Forgive for Good (Harris 2006). It is focused on forgiveness intervention studies. My understanding of this fascinating research is that the happiest people are those who give, the happiest of the happiest are those who forgive, and the least happy are those who carry a grudge. In one study, for example, the interventions focus on core components of forgiveness: taking less personal offense, blaming the offender less, and offering more personal and situational understanding of the offender and of oneself. Using techniques of cognitive behavioral therapy, mindfulness meditation, and guided imagery, the Stanford researchers used six sessions of 90 minutes each, spread out over six weeks. The researchers have concluded that skills-based forgiveness training may prove effective in reducing anger as a coping style, reducing stress and physical symptoms, and improving immune and cardiovascular functioning in daily living. Think of the implications for leaders as we learn more and more about how forgiveness works with our brains and our bodies. Leaders need ways to learn these insights and apply them to how they lead and how they live.

I believe that the best leaders are givers—and that this will be even truer in the future. The best leaders will be givers in long-term interpersonal relationships. Leaders will also give people an opportunity to give. That giving becomes one of the ways people get satisfaction, because it's not just money that motivates people. Part of the reward comes with how people feel when they give. I've spent quite a lot of time in Walt Disney World, for example, and I'm continuously impressed with the cast members, as the employees in the park are called. They are part of the play in the park, and their focus is on creating magical moments for the guests. The experience is delightful for the guests, but it is also a big positive for the cast members— far beyond the money that they are paid.

Leadership is not about winning in a way that other people lose. The future world of mutual-benefit partnering will be more about winning in a way that multiple people win. Adam Grant says it well in his book *Give & Take:*

> There's one group of givers, who are purely selfless, who constantly put other people's interests ahead of their own. But, there's this other group of givers that I call "otherish." They are concerned about benefitting others, but they also keep their own interests in the rearview mirror. They will look for ways to help others that are either low cost to themselves or even high benefit to themselves, i.e., "win-win," as opposed to win-

lose. Here's the irony. The selfless givers might be more altruistic, in principle, because they are constantly elevating other people's interests ahead of their own. But my data, and research by lots of others, show that they're actually less generous because they run out of energy, they run out of time and they lose their resources, because they basically don't take enough care of themselves. The "otherish" givers are able to sustain their giving by looking for ways that giving can hurt them less or benefit them more. (Grant 2013)

Most of the world's religions have a principle that relates to the importance of giving, but neuroscience is giving us new data to prove it.

Learning How to Lead at the Edge of Your Own Competence

In the future world we're all going to have to learn to live on the edge of our own competence. We're entering a decade in which the world will change so quickly and the challenges will be so unfamiliar that few will have proven competence. Most people will not be able to practice in the center of their competence, since such zones of stability will become increasingly rare.

Leaders will all have to learn how to fail gracefully at the edge of their competence, without pretending they know what they don't know. What can you do when you reach this edge of your own competency? In other words, how can you fail gracefully?

- Turn into a listener and ask lots of questions.
- Partner with somebody who knows more than you know in the space where you are weak.
- Bring in people who have different points of view than you have about spaces where you are strong.
- Set up a practice zone or prototyping environment where you can try out a number of things on a small scale (gaming for grit, as I call it in Chapters 3 and 4).
- Figure out a way to buy yourself some time to reflect and figure out what to do in this new space. Oftentimes you don't have to make a decision right away.

- Create a model to try to communicate the new topic. This is risky if you choose a model that doesn't work well.

The most dangerous thing you can do is to pretend that you know something that you actually don't know. Basically we all have to become skilled at failing successfully. Leaders must become even more competent at the edge of their own competence than they are in their specialties. In Silicon Valley, these experts are often referred to as T-Shaped People, who have depth but also breadth.*

Agility is all about transcendence and resilience. Agility is at the edge of your knowledge. If you're agile, you are not surprised by novelty. You confront the abyss with confidence, even though the rules are uncertain.

We are entering a decade when the world will be changing so quickly—and the challenges will be so unfamiliar—that few leaders will have a fully tested competence. Most leaders will play most of the time at the edge of their competence, and career well-being will require the resilience to fail gracefully at the edge of their own knowledge.

Seeding Hope in the Face of the VUCA World

As summarized in Figure 30, hope will be the key variable. Hope has always been important, but it is likely to be much more difficult to achieve over the next decade. You may get angry if you are not able to find a job, if you don't see a path forward. Some angry people will be financially pressured—in any ten-year forecast, the rich–poor gap will be stark—but their anger may be more about lack of hope than it is about economics. Even if you have shelter and food, people need hope.

I am a sociologist of religion by training, and in that field, we refer to "high-demand religions" as those that require a lot of their members but offer in return a sense of relief from uncertainty. Many terrorist groups practice this kind of religion: give us your life and your body; we will give

---

* The earliest reference I could find is David Guest, "The Hunt Is on for the Renaissance Man of Computing," in the *Independent*, September 17, 1991. I first heard this term from Tim Brown, the CEO of IDEO.

**Over the next decade, the biggest
negative disruptors will be**

young people who are hope*less*—and connected.

The biggest *positive* disruptors will be

young people who are hope*ful*—and connected.

The key variable will be

the degree of *hope*
young people experience.

FIGURE 30 Hope will be the key variable in a VUCA world.

you relief and purpose—either in this life or in the promised next life. Maybe what they offer is hard to perceive as hope, but at least is it relief.

Leaders in the future will be in the seeding hope business, whether they like it or not. Hope will be particularly important for those young people who became adults in 2010 or later, but gaming for grit (as discussed in Chapter 3) will help create both readiness and resilience:

> A fixed mindset about ability leads to pessimistic explanations of adversity, and that, in turn leads to both giving up on challenges and avoiding them in the first place. In contrast, a growth mindset leads to optimistic ways of explaining adversity, and that, in turn, leads to perseverance and seeking out new challenges that will ultimately make you even stronger. (Duckworth 2016)

The type of people who will succeed in shape-shifting organizations will be full of grit, hope, and optimism. It will be up to leaders to keep people hopeful and optimistic; in turn they will be rewarded with gritty people who will see adversity and change as an opportunity rather than a challenge.

One of my favorite book titles is *Just Enough Anxiety*, by Robert Rosen. So often, anxiety is viewed as a sickness or at least a condition that must be treated with drugs or therapy. In a VUCA world, however, anxiety will often be a normal and useful human response. Rosen opens his book with the famous Nelson Mandela quote: "The brave man is not he who does not feel afraid, but he who conquers that fear." Rosen then goes on to say:

> Anxiety is a fact of life. How you use it makes all the difference. If you let it overwhelm you, it will turn to panic. If you deny or run from it, you will become complacent. But if you use anxiety in a positive way, you will turn it into a powerful force in your life. (Rosen 2009)

Gamers already understand the value of anxiety. An epic win is preceded by anxiety before passing through to the other side.

When I was in divinity school, I was most attracted to Eastern religions. One of my favorite authors was the Zen philosopher Alan W. Watts, who wrote a book in 1951 that still seems so current today. It is called *The Wisdom of Insecurity: A Message for an Age of Anxiety*. It is weirdly comforting for me to think Watts and many others viewed 1951 as an "an age of anxiety," long before *the VUCA world* had been coined or experienced the way we do today. Certainly, leaders in the future will have the leadership literacy and the wisdom to lead with just enough—not *too* much—anxiety.

Figure 31 on the next page shows the process that leaders will need to follow to create positive energy.

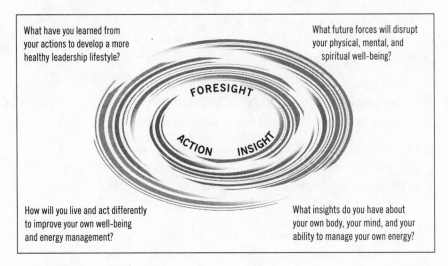

What have you learned from your actions to develop a more healthy leadership lifestyle?

What future forces will disrupt your physical, mental, and spiritual well-being?

FORESIGHT

ACTION   INSIGHT

How will you live and act differently to improve your own well-being and energy management?

What insights do you have about your own body, your mind, and your ability to manage your own energy?

FIGURE 31 The new literacy of creating positive energy, to seed realistic hope in a world laced with fear

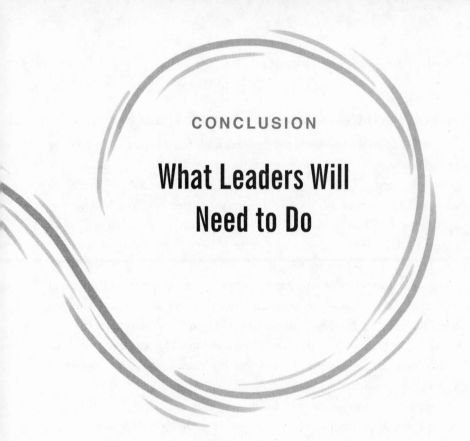

What Leaders Will Need to Do

AS I WAS FINISHING THIS BOOK, I HAD DINNER AT AMICI'S East Coast Pizzeria across the street from Draper University in my hometown of San Mateo, CA. It was especially busy that Sunday evening, and my waiter was being pulled in many directions by impatient and unfriendly customers. I noticed the pressure he was under, but I also noticed his calm. When I left, I gave him a large tip and a pat on the arm, saying I was impressed with his balance—in spite of the impatience around him. He thanked me for noticing and said, "You can't freak out. It's just a pizza restaurant." Leaders can't freak out either, especially if it's much more than a pizza restaurant.

Over the next decade, I'm confident that leaders will improve their leadership literacies that I've introduced in this book. Many leaders will become fluent—not just competent—in them. I hope that many of you will expand the lexicon and discover new literacies that I haven't imagined. The best literacies will turn into legacies for the next generation of leaders.

We Will Need New Literacies—beyond These Five

It is my job as an author to introduce new leadership literacies to you. By sharing my foresight about external future forces I'm urging you to draw out insights and actions for your own leadership. Leaders will make the future and I hope that this book will help you do just that. You will have to navigate what will be an increasingly VUCA world. It is your job as a leader to learn from these literacies as you see fit, expand them if you need to, and then turn them into your own legacies.

Legacies have taken on a new meaning in recent years with software and hardware legacies. Legacy systems are difficult to replace, even when they should be replaced. Legacy leadership should be difficult to replace because it is so widespread, so effective, and so compelling. The leadership legacies of distributed organizations are very much a work in progress now, but I expect great progress over the next decade.

I believe that the world will be increasingly turbulent over the next decade due to disruptions that will create breaks in the patterns of change, on a twisting path toward distributed everything. Distributed everything will mean disrupted everything. Four explosive ingredients will be at the root of these disruptions.

Globally, a large number of young people will be lacking in hope and unable to achieve a sense of meaning in their lives—*and* they will be very connected through digital media. The trigger for next-generation disruption will be a global boom of young people coming of age during a time that President Lyndon B. Johnson would have referred to as "the outskirts of hope."* I'm extremely optimistic about this next generation of young people, *if* they have hope. Hope is necessary for life. Kids are always striving to find hope and meaning. They have never before, however, been so connected while they searched for meaning. And I doubt that hope has ever been so hard to find for young people. In the near future, no matter how poor you are—even if you are hungry, homeless, and hopeless—you will

---

* President Lyndon B. Johnson said this in 1964: "Unfortunately, many Americans live on the outskirts of hope—some because of their poverty, and some because of their color, and all too many because of both. Our task is to help replace their despair with opportunity."

have access to good connectivity. What will be the shared sense of meaning for the next generation? Leaders must seed and nurture hope, especially in young people who are 21 or younger in 2017.

The gap between rich and poor will be oppressive—*and* increasingly visible. Extreme connectivity will be an opportunity to match workers to tasks that need to be done, but it will take great creativity and won't happen automatically. The poor kids will see the rich kids, in some cases, in high definition. Some of today's rich kids are flaunting their extreme wealth. The world has always had a rich-poor gap, but advanced connectivity will make the gap painfully visible.

Asymmetrical digital technology will enable terrorists to transmit data more quickly, which will make it easier to spread their message—*and* harder to control. Unpredictable violent disruptions will not be controlled by military means alone. You cannot just bomb them. The root economic and cultural dilemmas—like the rich-poor gap and the lack of hope that many people are experiencing—must be addressed in order to make a difference.

A world of continuous disruption will be too much for many people to process—*and* many people will be susceptible to simplistic and dangerous calls to action, especially from politicians and religious figures. Extreme religious and political movements are already recruiting young people— and this recruitment effort will become increasingly sophisticated in the future. Extreme groups will focus on youth who have little hope or meaning in their lives. Extremists will claim convincingly that they can solve the unsolvable for these young people. In turn, these simplistic attempts will spark spasmodic disruptions on top of the disruptions that youth are rebelling against. People who do not grow up with an inner sense of strength and orientation will be more shocked by external disruptions and more likely to turn to simplistic actions. When their inner strength gives out, many people will turn to external sources of strength—some of which will be much more dangerous than the threat to which they are responding.

Connectivity will mix the ingredients of disruption beyond what we imagine today, connectivity that is jerking us toward distributed everything. The threats of connectivity will be as flammable as gasoline, but there will also be opportunities. A sense of urgency will prevail, with many young leaders asking: why can't we make a difference now?

Those who became adults in 2010 or later will live and work in a world where media is so advanced that current social media pales in comparison.

Many of these young adults will be in leadership positions of power within the next decade. The digital media ecology in which they will be working will be characterized by the following advances:

- Social media will have robust social analytics and community-organizing capabilities. People marveled at how Facebook was used to help organize the first Arab Spring demonstrations, but that will look elementary.

- Much more graceful filtering capabilities will make it possible to have true blended-reality experiences that are spectacular by today's standards. While the details of the computer-human interfaces are still not clear, the smart phones and tablets of today will look crude in comparison. Google Glass was an early failure, but certainly we will look back and say it failed in an interesting way and that its successors will be much more graceful. Everyone who wants it will have a virtual overlay on the physical world.

- Video gaming interfaces will be even more vivid, with a much wider array of content. Interfaces like the ones used in video games will be ubiquitous, not just in video gaming but also in a very wide range of other applications.

- Gaming (or whatever it comes to be called) will evolve into the most powerful learning medium in history.

The future will be no ordinary world as today's young people become adults and join the workforce—whether they have a traditional job or find a more fluid way to make a living. The world of the future will demand so much more than is expected of leaders today. So many current leaders are still using ordinary leadership practices in pursuit of ordinary goals. Most of today's leaders were trained to solve problems, but they are flummoxed by dilemmas they cannot solve, dilemmas that won't go away.

Many leaders are not tuned to the multimedia world. Distributed media and shape-shifting organizations will disrupt every industry. The disruptive shift from technology to media will alter the nature of leadership. It will require new leadership disciplines, new leadership practices, and new leadership literacies. The key amplifier will be radical connectivity.

What will be new will be the scale of disruption: leaders will have to deal with disruption on a global scale—because of the super connectivity that we all experience. Global disruption will be loaded with dilemmas. It will be a frightening future, but it also will be a hopeful future.

This book is grounded in foresight, which is a particularly good way to provoke insight. Insight, as I discussed in detail in Chapter 1, is an aha moment that alters your view. Insight draws new connections in your brain. Once you have an insight, you can't go back to your old way of thinking. Insight changes you.

Leaders will need new insight about how to be resilient in the face of next-generation disruption and dilemmas. We need to make some sense out of disruptive dilemmas that often seem to make no sense at all. We can start by learning from other parts of the world around us, the parts that seem so far away to many Americans.

Andrew Solomon's recent book documents his life as a journalist traveling to highly uncertain parts of the world—such as Libya, Brazil, Antarctica, and Myanmar—in ways that immersed him in the local culture way beyond what a tourist would experience. Traveling to the future should be like Solomon describes his own experiences in distant lands:

> You cannot understand the otherness of places you have not encountered. If all young adults were required to spend two weeks in a foreign country, two-thirds of the world's diplomatic problems could be solved. It wouldn't matter what country they visited or what they did during their stays. They would simply need to come to terms with the existence of other places, and recognize that people live differently there—that some phenomena are universal and others culturally particular. (Solomon 2016)

Fewer than half of Americans have passports, and only 10 percent of Americans travel out of the country each year. Out of all the United States, New Jersey has the most passport holders (62 percent), and Mississippi has the fewest (18 percent) (International Trade Administration 2015). Do most Americans really understand the outside world of the present, let alone the future? Leaders will need to come to terms with the otherness of not only

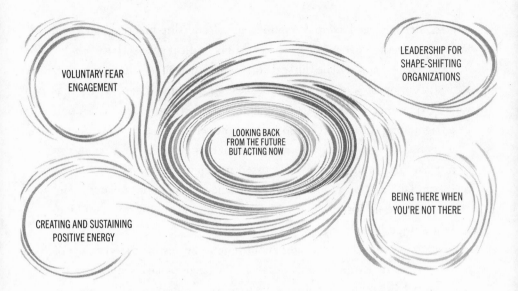

FIGURE 32 The New Leadership Literacies

other countries but also other futures. Fear of others who are different is largely based in a lack of exposure. Gameful engagement, as I discussed in Chapter 3, can help by immersing leaders in different worlds with different people—all in ways that are compelling and personal but low risk.

If you haven't experienced something, it is easy to fear that something. And if you don't know particular kinds or categories of people, they might seem scary to you. But until you have experienced or met them, you will never know. And isn't engagement much more attractive than isolation?

This book looks ten years ahead but pulls back hard to draw out practical insights for leaders—and everyday people—in the present. The future will be a world of disruption *and* a world of disruptive opportunity. Leaders will need to travel to alternative futures.

Leaders will need voluntary fear exposure, not only to learn how to live with fear but also to learn how to flip that fear into opportunity. They will need safe zones (think games, simulations, or immersive experiences) to try out their future leadership skills in low-risk settings. They will need new ways to partner in guilds or communities, so they don't have to go it alone. They will need new media savvy to lead through the rich mix of media that is just coming to life. And finally, leaders will need to be physically, mentally, and spiritually fit in ways that were never required before.

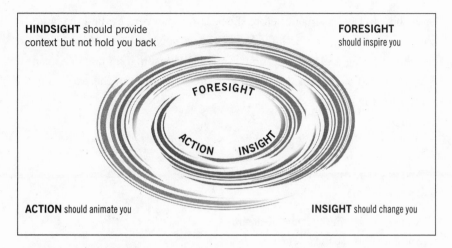

HINDSIGHT should provide context but not hold you back

FORESIGHT should inspire you

FORESIGHT

ACTION INSIGHT

ACTION should animate you

INSIGHT should change you

FIGURE 33 Leaders will need to draw from all literacies to seed hope.

We all have to find ways of making sense out of the VUCA world, but the VUCA world will be too complicated for many people. As leaders we have to recognize that people around us are likely to become trapped in simplistic thinking, particularly as practiced in politics and religion. Will there be leadership voices loud enough or quietly comforting enough to quell people's fear?

Leaders will need to lead while not going over what I call the threshold of righteousness. It's one thing to believe you're right and have clarity about a future direction. It's quite another to believe everybody else is wrong. Clarity can degrade into certainty.

You, as leaders in a dilemma-ridden world, will have to figure out how to thrive in this space between judging too soon (the classic mistake of the problem solver) and deciding too late (the classic mistake of the academic). I believe that the next ten years will be twisted and splintered—the most turbulent years in all of our lifetimes—*and* the most hopeful, if we play it right.

Hope will be the key variable. Hope will be especially important for young people, those 21 years old or younger in 2017. Leaders will need to seed hope in a fashion suggested by Figure 33.

As I was finishing this book, I had dinner with my wife Robin, and we were talking about the importance of hope over the next decade in particular. Robin, an English major before she became a lawyer, recalled the famous line "'Hope' is the thing with feathers," and we spent the rest of our evening together reading and talking about Emily Dickinson. The new leadership literacies need to be spiced with this poetic wisdom from the past, to prepare us for the future.

"Hope" is the thing with feathers—
That perches in the soul—
And sings the tune without the words—
And never stops—at all—

And sweetest—in the Gale—is heard—
And sore must be the storm—
That could abash the little Bird
That kept so many warm—

I've heard it in the chilliest land—
And on the strangest Sea—
Yet, never, in Extremity,
It asked a crumb—of Me.
  (Dickinson 1891)

This next decade will ask a lot more than "a crumb" from leaders. Leaders *will* be distributed, whether they like it or not. Centralized organizations and authoritarian personalities constrained by certainty will not succeed in a world twisting toward distributed everything. It will be up to leaders— and there will be lots of them in a shape-shifting world—to make a hopeful future.

FUTURE READINESS
SELF-ASSESSMENT

THE SELF-ASSESSMENT ASKS YOU TO COMPLETE A candid evaluation of where you stand with regard to each of the five future literacies introduced in this book, as well as the ten future leadership skills introduced in *Leaders Make the Future.* The challenge I hope you will take away from reading this book is how to apply this foresight to provoke your own insights and actions—to make yourself a better leader. I am giving you a process you can use to develop yourself as a leader.

An important step in this process is the Future Leadership Literacies & Skills Self-Assessment, which is a companion product to this book and is available on the Berrett-Koehler web site:

www.bkconnection.com/leaderliteraciesskills-sa

The self-assessment is a very useful starting point for individuals, but it is also a great conversation starter for workshops and team-building events. I often use it with groups before my talks or workshops. Bulk-order discounts are also available for organizational programs.

The self-assessment is a chance to reflect on yourself and your leadership—given the external future forces of the next decade. In a world where everything that can be distributed will be distributed, are you ready to lead the kind of shape-shifting organizations that will become possible?

BIBLIOGRAPHY

Abidi, Suhayl, and Manoj Joshi. *The VUCA Company: How Indian Companies Have Faced Volatility, Uncertainty, Complexity & Ambiguity.* Fort, Mumbai: Jaico House, 2015. Print.

Anderson, Robert J., and W.A. Adams. *Mastering Leadership: An Integrated Framework for Breakthrough Performance and Extraordinary Business Results.* Hoboken, NJ: Wiley, 2016. Print.

The Arbringer Institute, trans. *The Outward Mindset: Seeing beyond Ourselves.* Oakland, CA: Berrett-Koehler, 2016. Print.

Ariely, Dan, and Matt R. Trower. *Payoff: The Hidden Logic That Shapes Our Motivations.* London: TED, 2016. Print.

Baker, Wayne E. *Achieving Success through Social Capital: Tapping the Hidden Resources in Your Personal and Business Networks.* San Francisco: Jossey-Bass, 2000. Print.

Barbeck-Letmathe, Peter. *Nutrition for a Better Life: A Journey from the Origins of Industrial Food Production to the Nutrigenomic Diet of the Future.* Frankfurt/New York: Campus Verlag, 2016. Print.

Birtles, Bill. "China's Narcissistic Social Media Stars Making $20k per Month." N.p., 26 July 2016. Web.

Bodell, Lisa. *Why Simple Wins: Escape the Complexity Trap and Get to Work That Matters*. Brookline, MA: Bibliomotion, 2017. Print.

Boyd, Danah. *It's Complicated: The Social Lives of Networked Teens*. New Haven, CT: Yale UP, 2015. Print.

Brown, Brené. *Daring Greatly: How the Courage to Be Vulnerable Transforms the Way We Live, Love, Parent, and Lead*. London: Penguin, 2016. Print.

Brown, Tim, and Barry Katz. *Change by Design: How Design Thinking Transforms Organizations and Inspires Innovation*. New York: Harper Business, 2011. Print.

Burton, Robert. *A Skeptic's Guide to the Mind: What Neuroscience Can and Cannot Tell Us about Ourselves*. New York: St. Martin's Griffin, 2014. Print.

Chamorro-Premuzic, Tomas. "Does Money Really Affect Motivation? A Review of the Research." *Harvard Business Review* April 10, 2013. https://hbr.org/2013/04/does-money-really-affect-motiv.

Christian, Brian. *The Most Human Human: What Artificial Intelligence Teaches Us about Being Alive*. New York: Anchor, 2012. Print.

Cialdini, Robert B. *Influence: The Psychology of Persuasion*. New York: Collins, n.d. Print.

Collins, James C., and Morten T. Hansen. *Great by Choice: Uncertainty, Chaos, and Luck—Why Some Thrive Despite Them All*. New York: Harper Business, 2011. Print.

Danskin, Karl, and Jenny Lind. *Virtuous Meetings: Technology Design for High Engagement in Large Groups*. San Francisco: Jossey Bass, 2014. Print.

Darling, Marilyn, Charles Parry, and Joseph Moore. "Learning in the Thick of It." *Harvard Business Review*. July–August, 2005.

Dhawan, Erica, and Saj-nicole A. Joni. *Get Big Things Done: The Power of Connectional Intelligence*. New York: Palgrave Macmillan Trade, 2015. Print.

Dickinson, Emily, and Thomas Herbert Johnson. *The Complete Poems of Emily Dickinson*. Boston: Little, Brown, 2015. Print.

Dweck, Carol S. *Mindset*. London: Robinson, an Imprint of Constable & Robinson, 2017. Print.

Economist. "Generation Uphill." January 23, 2016.

Flieger, Verlyn. *Splintered Light: Logos and Language in Tolkien's World*. Grand Rapids, MI: Wm. B. Eerdmans, 1983. Print.

Friedman, Thomas L. *Thank You for Being Late: An Optimist's Guide to Thriving in the Age of Accelerations*. Waterville, ME: Thorndike Large Print, 2017. Print.

Gans, Joshua. *Disruption Dilemma*. Cambridge, MA: MIT, 2017. Print.

Ghaemi, S. Nassir. *A First-Rate Madness: Uncovering the Links between Leadership and Mental Illness*. New York: Penguin, 2012. Print.

Gilmore, James H. *Look: A Practical Guide for Improving Your Observational Skills*. Austin, TX: Greenleaf Book Group, 2016. Print.

Hallenbeck, George. *Learning Agility*. Greensboro: Center for Creative Leadership, 2016. Print.

Harari, Yuval N. *Sapiens: A Brief History of Humankind*. Toronto, Ontario: Signal, McClelland & Stewart, 2016. Print.

Harris, Michael. *The End of Absence: Reclaiming What We've Lost in a World of Constant Connection*. New York: Doubleday, 2014. Print.

Haven, Kendall F. *Story Smart: Using the Science of Story to Persuade, Influence, Inspire, and Teach*. Santa Barbara, CA: Libraries Unlimited, 2014. Print.

Hochschild, Arlie Russell. *Strangers in Their Own Land: A Journey to the Heart of the American Right*. New York: New Press, 2016. Print.

Hock, Dee. *Birth of the Chaordic Age*. San Francisco, CA: Berrett-Koehler, 1999. Print.

Hoffman, Bryce. *American Icon: Alan Mulally and the Fight to Save Ford Motor Company*. New York: Crown, 2013.

IBM. *Device Democracy*. Rep. IBM, July 2015. Web.

International Trade Administration, U.S. Resident Travel to International Destinations Increased Nine Percent in 2015, 24 Feb. 2016. Web.

Ismail, Salim, M. Malone, and Peter H. Diamandis. *Exponential Organizations: Why New Organizations Are Ten Times Better, Faster, and Cheaper Than Yours (and What to Do about It)*. New York: Diversion, 2014. Print.

Ito, Mizuko. *Hanging Out, Messing Around, and Geeking Out*. Cambridge, MA: MIT, 2013. Print.

Jenkins, Bruce. *SF Chronicle* 6 June 2016: B9. Print.

Johansen, Bob. *Get There Early: Sensing the Future to Compete in the Present*. San Francisco: Berrett-Koehler, 2007. Print.

———. *Leaders Make the Future: Ten New Leadership Skills for an Uncertain World*. San Francisco: Berrett-Koehler, 2012. Print.

Johansen, Bob, and Karl Ronn. *Reciprocity Advantage*. San Francisco: Berrett-Koehler, 2014. Print.

Johansen, Robert. *Groupware: Computer Support for Business Teams*. New York: Free Press, 1988. Print.

Johansen, Robert, and Rob Swigart. *Upsizing the Individual in the Downsized Organization: Managing in the Wake of Reengineering, Globalization, and Overwhelming Technological Change*. Reading, MA: Addison-Wesley, 1995. Print.

Johnson, Steven. *Everything Bad Is Good for You: How Popular Culture Is Making Us Smarter*. London: Penguin, 2006. Print.

Johnston, Douglas. *Faith-based Diplomacy: Trumping Realpolitik*. Oxford: Oxford UP, 2008. Print.

Kaplan, Jerry. *Humans Need Not Apply: A Guide to Wealth and Work in the Age of Artificial Intelligence*. New Haven: Yale UP, 2015. Print.

Kean, Sam. *The Tale of the Dueling Neurosurgeons: The History of the Human Brain as Revealed by True Stories of Trauma, Madness, and Recovery*. New York: Little, Brown, 2014. Print.

Keen, Andrew. *Digital Vertigo: How Today's Online Social Revolution Is Dividing, Diminishing, and Disorienting Us*. New York: St. Martin's Griffin, 2013. Print.

Kelley, Tom, and David Kelley. *Creative Confidence: Unleashing the Creative Potential within Us All*. London: William Collins, 2015. Print.

Kelly, Kevin. *The Inevitable: Understanding the 12 Technological Forces That Will Shape Our Future*. New York: Viking, 2016. Print.

Keltner, Dacher. *The Power Paradox: How We Gain and Lose Influence*. New York: Penguin, 2016. Print.

Kilcullen, David. *Accidental Guerrilla*. New York: Oxford UP, 2009. Print.

Kirshbaum, Jeremy Joe. "Cultural Comparative Advantage and Network Thinking in Ghana." *BizzAfrica*. July 26, 2013. http://www.bizzafrica.com/posts/36.

Klein, Gary. *Sources of Power: How People Make Decisions*. Cambridge, MA: MIT, 2015. Print.

Krishna, Golden. *The Best Interface Is No Interface: The Simple Path to Brilliant Technology*. San Francisco, CA: New Riders, 2015. Print.

Krupp, Steven, Paul J. H. Schoemaker, and David J. Teece. *Winning the Long Game: How Strategic Leaders Shape the Future*. New York: Public Affairs, 2014. Print.

Le Guin, Ursula K. *A Fisherman of the Inland Sea*, 1994. In James Gleick, *Time Travel: A History*, p 273. New York: Pantheon Books, 2016. Print.

Lewis, Michael. *The Undoing Project: A Friendship That Changed Our Minds*. New York: W.W. Norton, 2017. Print.

Marshall, S. L. A. *Men against Fire: The Problem of Battle Command*. Norman, OK: University of Oklahoma Press, 2000. Print.

Masahiro Mori. "The Uncanny Valley: The Original Essay by Masahiro Mori." 12 June 2012. Web.

McChrystal, Stanley A. *My Share of the Task: A Memoir*. New York: Portfolio/Penguin, 2014. Print.

McChrystal, Stanley A., Tantum Collins, David Silverman, and Chris Fussell. *Team of Teams: New Rules of Engagement for a Complex World*. New York: Portfolio/Penguin, 2015. Print.

McGonigal, Jane. *Reality Is Broken: Why Games Make Us Better and How They Can Change the World*. London: Vintage, 2012. Print.

Mullainathan, Sendhil, and Eldar Shafir. *Scarcity: Why Having Too Little Means So Much*. New York: Picador, Henry Holt, 2014. Print.

Page, Scott E. *The Difference: How the Power of Diversity Creates Better Groups, Firms, Schools, and Societies*. Princeton, NJ: Princeton UP, 2008. Print.

Palfrey, John G., and Urs Gasser. *Born Digital: Understanding the First Generation of Digital Natives*. Sydney: Read How You Want, 2011. Print.

Parisi, Tony. *Learning Virtual Reality: Developing Immersive Experiences and Applications for Desktop, Web, and Mobile*. Beijing: O'Reilly, 2016. Print.

Pendleton-Jullian, Ann M., and John Seely Brown. *Pragmatic Imagination: Single from Design Unbound*. San Francisco, CA: Blurb (self-publishing platform), 2016. Print.

Pfeffer, Jeffrey. *Leadership BS: Fixing Workplaces and Careers One Truth at a Time*. New York: Harper Business, an Imprint of HarperCollins, 2015. Print.

Pietersen, Willie. *Reinventing Strategy: Using Strategic Learning to Create and Sustain Breakthrough Performance*. New York: Wiley & Sons, 2002. Print.

Pike, John. "Military." Web.

Piketty, Thomas, and Arthur Goldhammer. *Capital in the Twenty-first Century*. Cambridge, MA: Belknap of Harvard UP, 2014. Print.

Prothero, Stephen R. *God Is Not One: The Eight Rival Religions That Run the World—and Why Their Differences Matter*. New York: HarperOne, 2010. Print.

Putnam, Robert David. *Our Kids: The American Dream in Crisis*. New York: Simon & Schuster Paperbacks, 2016. Print.

Quick, Larry, David Platt, and Kristin Van Vloten. *Disrupted: Strategy for Exponential Change*. Woodend, Victoria: Resilient Futures Media, 2015. Print.

Rich, Frederic C. *Getting to Green: Saving Nature, a Bipartisan Solution*. New York: W.W. Norton, 2016. Print.

Rock, David. *Your Brain at Work: Strategies for Overcoming Distraction, Regaining Focus, and Working Smarter All Day Long*. New York: HarperCollins, 2009. Print.

Rogers, Everett M., and Judith K. Larsen. *Silicon Valley Fever: Growth of High-technology Culture*. New York: Basic, 1984. Print.

Rose, David. *Enchanted Objects: Design, Human Desire, and the Internet of Things*. New York: Scribner, 2014. Print.

Rosen, Robert H. *Just Enough Anxiety: The Hidden Driver of Business Success*. New York: Portfolio, 2008. Print.

Ross, Alec. *Industries of the Future*. New York: Simon & Schuster, 2017. Print.

Rothkopf, David J. *National Insecurity: American Leadership in an Age of Fear*. New York: Public Affairs, 2016. Print.

Sandberg, Sheryl. *Lean In*. New York: Alfred A. Knopf, a division of Random House, 2013. Print.

Shedroff, Nathan, and Christopher Noessel. *Make It So: Interaction Design Lessons from Science Fiction*. Brooklyn, NY: Rosenfeld Media, 2012. Print.

Sheridan, Richard. *Joy, Inc.: How We Built a Workplace People Love.* New York: Portfolio/Penguin, 2015. Print.

Sibbet, David. *Visual Leaders: New Tools for Visioning, Management, and Organization Change.* Hoboken: John Wiley & Sons, 2013. Print.

Smick, David M. *The Great Equalizer: How Main Street Capitalism Can Create an Economy for Everyone.* New York: PublicAffairs, 2017. Print.

Smiley, Tavis, and David Ritz. *Death of a King: The Real Story of Dr. Martin Luther King Jr.'s Final Year.* New York: Little, Brown, 2014. Print.

Stefik, Mark. "The Next Knowledge Medium." *AI Magazine* 7, no. 1 (1986).

————. *Internet Dreams: Archetypes, Myths, and Metaphors.* Cambridge, MA: MIT, 2001. Print.

————. *The Internet Edge: Social, Technical, and Legal Challenges for a Networked World.* Cambridge, MA: MIT, 2000. Print.

Stefik, Mark, and Barbara Stefik. *Breakthrough: Stories and Strategies of Radical Innovation.* Cambridge, MA: MIT, 2006. Print.

Taleb, Nassim Nicholas. *Antifragile: Things That Gain from Disorder.* New York: Random House Trade Paperbacks, 2014. Print.

Tapscott, Don. *Growing up Digital: The Rise of the Net Generation.* New York: McGraw-Hill, 2000. Print.

Tapscott, Don, and Alex Tapscott. *Blockchain Revolution: How the Technology behind Bitcoin Is Changing Money, Business and the World.* New York: Portfolio/Penguin, 2016. Print.

Traver, Kelly, and Betty Kelly Sargent. *The Healthiest You: Take Charge of Your Brain to Take Charge of Your Life.* New York: Atria Paperback, 2011. Print.

Turkle, Sherry. *Alone Together: Why We Expect More from Technology and Less from Each Other.* Cambridge, MA: Perseus, 2013. Print.

————. *Reclaiming Conversation: The Power of Talk in a Digital Age.* New York: Penguin, an Imprint of Penguin Random House LLC, 2016. Print.

Wachter, Robert M. *The Digital Doctor: Hope, Hype, and Harm at the Dawn of Medicine's Computer Age.* New York: McGraw-Hill Education, 2017. Print.

Watts, Alan. *The Wisdom of Insecurity.* New York: Pantheon 1951. Print.

Webb, Amy. *The Signals Are Talking: Why Today's Fringe Is Tomorrow's Mainstream.* New York: PublicAffairs, 2017. Print.

Webb, Maynard, and Carlye Adler. *Rebooting Work: Transform How You Work in the Age of Entrepreneurship.* San Francisco: Jossey-Bass, 2013. Print.

Yorke, John. *Into the Woods: A Five-Act Journey into Story.* New York: Overlook, 2015. Print.

ACKNOWLEDGMENTS

THIS IS THE MOST PERSONAL BOOK I'VE EVER WRITTEN.
It didn't start that way, but over the three years I've been working on it, I realized that the digital tools for distributed everything have been unfolding in parallel to my own career path. At each key stage, it seemed like I had a personal story that brought it together for me—and now, I hope, for readers. I'm not saying I was in the center of these disruptive shifts, but I certainly had an interesting view.

Writing such a personal book makes me feel so thankful for all those with whom I have worked along this long journey. I got to spend an afternoon with Peter Drucker in his living room during the last year of his life. I was there with A.G. Lafley, when he was the CEO of Procter & Gamble, and our topic was the future of human resources. I still remember Peter Drucker advising that you should do many different things and work with many different kinds of people early in your life, because you don't yet know who you are. At age 94, Peter Drucker told us that for the second half of your life, you should work only on things you are passionate about and only with people with whom you love to work. At this stage in my life, I've reached the Drucker goal where I'm working only on things I'm passionate about and mostly with people with whom I love to work.

My path began in Geneva, Illinois—a small farming town where most everyone loved basketball, including me. Two coaches, Mel Johnson and Bob Schick, were inspiring for me at a time when I was more coachable than teachable. My best friend from high school, Bob Liden, continues to inspire me with his fighting spirit that somehow retains a sparkle-in-the-eye friendliness. Strength with humility, I call it now. Ken Carder was my youth minister in Geneva, and he took me to Washington, DC and New York City for the first time. A civil rights marcher, Ken taught me things that I wasn't ready to learn until much later. My parents, Randy and Evelyn, were the grounding for everything in my life. Even though they didn't attend college, they encouraged me to go as far as I wanted with my education. Their values, particularly with regard to reciprocity, still pervade my life. My sister Jeanie taught me about generosity.

My best friend from my undergraduate experience at the University of Illinois in Champaign-Urbana is Rock Anderson, the first engineer I knew well. I now understand that Rock has a very strong strain of environmental engineering as well. Bio-empathy, I call it now. Much of my career has involved working with engineers and scientists, so Rock was an important beginning. Also at Illinois, I reached my maximum level of performance as a basketball player (it did pay my way through college), but more importantly, I met my wife, Robin. My time with Robin is the most special experience in my life as we continue to grow together. Everything in my life begins with Robin.

While Robin taught high school English and film, I went off to divinity school, fascinated with religion but not feeling any call to the ministry or to any brand of church. My look-and-see fellowship fueled that curiosity without constraint. Divinity school taught me how to systematically study the dilemmas of religion during a period of great turmoil and social change—the late '60s. The divinity school shared a campus with the Martin Luther King School of Social Change, which was supported largely by the Quakers. My professors were life-changing for me. Art Shostak introduced me to the discipline of sociology and the systematic study of the future. His excitement as a speaker and teacher lives on in me today. I became a research assistant to Jesse Brown, professor of Old Testament by training, but one who also focused on the modern arts and social change. I shared an office with him and marveled at how he worked in that small office with floor-to-ceiling bookshelves. I have an office a lot like that now at home. Ken Cauthen, a theologian at the intersection of religion and science, gave me the chance to support him at a conference on religion and the future, where I was able to meet many of the world's leading futurists at the time. Herb Williams, a professor in the King School, pushed me to the edge in my thinking about social change movements—but pulled me back before I went over the edge. Fellow student Fred Hodkins introduced the discipline of philosophy to me with great excitement, and he taught me how to play guitar. I see now that they are quite related.

When I went to Northwestern for my PhD program, something really big started: the internet (then called the ARPANET). I was completely taken by the social issues of networked connectivity. My professors at Northwestern were wonderful. Taylor and June McConnell, Rocky Smith, Donald T. Campbell, Carol Owen, and Jim Schuyler particularly influenced me. I did teach sociology of religion and introduction to sociology full-time for one year before realizing that I needed to be focused on the future. Somehow, through good timing and luck, I ended up in Silicon Valley (before it was called that) and at Institute for the Future, a unique shape-shifting organization that has prospered for nearly 50 years. I am so grateful to Roy Amara, then president of IFTF, for taking a chance on me.

When I arrived, I worked for Jacques Vallee on a team to develop prototype social media for scientists and engineers on the ARPANET. I was asked recently to name the most future-oriented leader I had ever worked for; I answered Jacques Vallee. When I arrived in Silicon Valley, I met Doug Engelbart, the father of the mouse, the windows interface, screen-sharing, hyper-media, and a wide range of other concepts that Silicon Valley is still chasing. Doug's vision was *so* big that I was humbled—and I still am. He had a real gentleness about him. Strength with humility.

About the same time, I met David Sibbet, the father of group graphic recording—which has now evolved into visual thinking and visual storytelling. I have worked with David in so many different venues, and I'm now working with visual recorders and visual storytellers who were trained by

David. David has shaped how I think about and visualize the future. David's spiritual grounding is a critical part of his work and his life.

When we arrived in Silicon Valley, Robin went to Stanford Law School and while she was there, I got to take a "spouses course" intended to teach us just enough about the law to live with a lawyer. I am so appreciative for that course and for Robin's experience at Stanford, which I got to share.

I've had a series of distinct careers at Institute for the Future, an independent nonprofit research organization. First, I led social evaluations for early social media being used by scientists. Then, I tried unsuccessfully to develop a new research program on learning in the future. Then, I started our first cost-shared research program with corporate support, a program that is still going strong. Next, I became the IFTF president for eight years during both the boom and bubble burst in Silicon Valley. Now I do custom forecasts for individual organizations, I write books, and I give talks. I love what I do, and I'm so thankful for all the people over the years at IFTF who have allowed me to do it. Marina Gorbis leads IFTF so well, and she has given me great support to do what I'm doing. Marina also has encouraged me to have a personal research assistant who is different from me in an interesting way. We rotate this role about every two years and I have been so blessed by the young people who have found me and from whom I have learned so much: Matt Chwierut, Rachel Lyle Hatch, Deepa Mehta, Alessandro Voto, Jeremy Kirshbaum, and now Sebastian Benitez. Jeremy Kirshbaum has been extremely helpful in teaching me about innovations in Africa and how they apply to future leadership literacies. Reverse or multi-directional mentoring may be the most powerful way to learn in the VUCA world, and it is certainly very useful for me.

Susanne Forchheimer helped me get started on a strong footing until she went on to another role at IFTF and Sebastian Benitez stepped in. Sebastian deserves special thanks since he has been focused on this book for more than one year. He is both a gifted futurist and a serious gamer. Chapters 3 and 4 benefitted greatly from my many discussions with him. Sebastian is 26 years old and a lifelong gamer and—more importantly—he sees gaming as a learning medium. I first got interested in gaming when I was in divinity school and I co-authored a role-play game called Spinoff with Garry Shirts, Jacques Vallee, and Kathi Vian (then Spangler) that was published in our book called *Electronic Meetings: Technical Alternatives and Social Choices.* But I am not a gamer the way Sebastian is a gamer. Sebastian loves to play video games—and almost any other games—but more importantly for this book, he helped me think through the potential of gaming as a learning medium for leadership development. Andy Billings at Electronic Arts has gone further than anyone else in the corporate world toward bringing this powerful new learning medium to life.

A special thanks to Ben Hammamoto at IFTF, who introduced me to Miku—the crowd-sourced virtual Japanese pop-music sensation. Ben is a soft-spoken storyteller with remarkable instincts for a good story that stretches thinking about the future. Together, we were able to bring out the story of Miku that I tell in this book. Miku is teaching leaders how they can embody their workers in an augmented future world.

When I began this book three years ago, Laurel Funkhouser was my assistant to manage my calendar and help me prioritize. Now Ashley Hemstreet plays that role, and I am so grateful. Managing my calendar has never been my strong suit, but I feel so blessed to have such skilled and knowledgeable colleagues. Sean Ness arranges many of my talks and helps me prioritize and draw links to other efforts at IFTF. Without Ashley and Sean, I would truly be overwhelmed and far less productive.

The IFTF production team has been awesome in helping me express my ideas through visuals. I tested the core ideas in this book through a long series of talks over a period of three years. In a real sense, the earliest drafts of the book were written in PowerPoint. Jean Hagan, Robin Bogott, Lisa Mumbach, and Trent Kuhn were so helpful. The IFTF production team contributed core graphics to Archie Ferguson, my absolute favorite book cover designer.

The collegial mood at Institute for the Future gets better every year. Now, our core staff skews young, female, and international. I am on the road much of the time, but when I'm at IFTF I sit in the coffee shop area and have spontaneous conversations that are always so provocative and interesting. It is just fun to be at IFTF, both physically and virtually. I think that almost any idea I have traces back to something I learned at IFTF. IFTF's additional current core staff and close affiliates, beyond those I've already mentioned, include

Richard Adler	Alexander Goldman	Jerry Michalski
Miriam Avery	David Evan Harris	Eric Moore
Cindy Baskin	Rachel Hatch	Carol Neuschul
Jamais Cascio	Dylan Hendricks	Ben Oppenheim
Rebecca Chesney	Toshi Hoo	David Pescovitz
Matt Chwierut	Parminder Jassal	Howard Rheingold
Tom Conger	Lyn Jeffery	Christina Rupp
Peter Coughlan	Pardeep Johal	Doug Rushkoff
Mattia Crespi	Andy Keller	Katherine Sanstad
Jake Dunagan	Maureen Kirchner	Sara Skvirsky
Jan English-Lueck	Brad Kreit	Sarah Smith
Rod Falcon	Trent Kuhn	Jason Tester
Devin Fidler	Daria Lamb	David Thigpen
Tessa Finlev	Neela Lazkani	Andrew Trabulsi
Natalie Foster	Mike Liebhold	Alessandro Voto
Mark Frauenfelder	Mary Kay Magistad	Ariel Waldman
Katie Fuller	Rachel Maguire	Salley Westergaard
Eri Gentry	Jane McGonigal	Nic Widinger

The IFTF board has played such an important role over the years and we are so fortunate to have these volunteer efforts. IFTF's external board members include Berit Ashla, Karen Edwards, Marianne Jackson, Michael Kleeman, Steve Milovich, and Lawrence Wilkinson.

Kathleen Vian has been a long-term thinking partner for almost everything I've done. She writes and thinks much better than I do, but I have been able to learn and apply our discussions in different ways. She has not yet seen this book, but I'm sure she will get it immediately.

I've learned so much from the talks I've given at a wide range of organizations as the ideas in this book have taken shape. In particular, thanks so much to General Mills, P&G, Aetna, CIGNA, National Defense University, PepsiCo, Frito Lay, Purina, Nestlé, Kellogg's, Luxottica, Hallmark, Microsoft, ASDA, Walmart, US Army War College, 3M, McKinsey, Stanford, University of Michigan, Center for Creative Leadership, Campbell's Soup, Humana, Teva, Zenity, Deloitte University, Coro Foundation, Colgate Palmolive, Hills Pet Science, PetSmart, SEIU, AFSCME, Northwell Health, UPS, Intel,

First Pacific, Sodexo, WhiteWave Foods, Center for Corporate Innovation, Syngenta, Consortium of Endowed Parishes (Episcopal Church), University of Texas, The Leadership Circle, Information Technology Senior Manager's Forum, Hyundai, AMA, MES (CEO Forum), Association of Managers of Innovation, Thayer Leadership Development Group at West Point, Betsy Magness Graduate Institute (Women in Cable Telecommunications), Cox Enterprises, Texas Children's Hospital, Boston University Executive Development Round Table, Executive and Board Symposium.

Shortly after I joined Institute for the Future, I got a call out of the blue from Ray Cartier and Bill Griebstein from Procter & Gamble. They were trying to make sense out of the ARPANET as a way to connect their scientists globally. I have worked continuously with P&G people since then, serving as a kind of outpost in Silicon Valley. Out of all the companies I have worked with over the years, the most important things that I've done almost always link back one way or the other to P&G. Mark Schar was one of our strongest advocates at P&G and, after he retired from P&G, Mark, Elizabeth Schar, and I did one of my favorite projects ever on the future of fun at Walt Disney World. Karl Ronn helped me write about the lessons from that work in our book *The Reciprocity Advantage.* I am a futurist, focused ten years ahead. Karl, and so many others with P&G roots, have the amazing ability to learn from foresight, but turn it into insight and action. I continue working with our former P&G client Robert Scott, who is now Dean of the Information Technology Senior Manager's Forum—the largest mentoring network for African American IT leaders. Robert has contributed greatly to this group, particularly the chapter on shape-shifting organizations and the importance of diversity as a source of innovation.

After writing six other books with large publishers, I started working with Berrett-Koehler on *Get There Early* in 2007. Since then, I've written two editions of *Leaders Make the Future* and cowritten *The Reciprocity Advantage* with Karl Ronn. Working with BK is unlike any other publishing experience I have had. It is more like a family than a corporation, although there is a constant clarity about "connecting people and ideas to create a world that works for all." Steve Piersanti is my editor and he has taught me what an editor should be: tough, relentless, and positive at just the right times. I have had many calls and meetings with Steve and I always feel exhausted—until

Steve concludes that the book is done and the message is clear. What a gift to be able to work with Steve.

The staff at BK work together so seamlessly that I sometimes don't know just who does what. I am so grateful to them all: Maria Jesus Aguilo, Charlotte Ashlock, Shabnam Banerjee-McFarland, Leslie Crandell, Michael Crowley, James Faani, Matt Fagaly, Kristen Frantz, Arielle Kesweder, Anna Leinberger, Catherine Lengronne, Zoe Mackey, Neal Maillet, David Marshall, Elizabeth McKellar, Kate Piersanti, M.J. Ramos, Anders Renee, Courtney Schonfeld, Katie Sheehan, Jeevan Sivasubramaniam, Jason VanDenEng, Johanna Vondeling, Edward Wade, Lasell Whipple, Rosalee White, and Ginger Winters.

Dave Peattie and Tanya Grove worked with me, as they have for my last four books, on the final editing and production. What an amazing team! I am humbled by what Dave and Tanya are able to do to bring my rough text to life and—I hope—clarity for readers. Tanya is certainly the best copy editor I have ever had. She has challenged me at each stage and pressed me to say it just right.

My writing of this book was partially supported by the Center for Creative Leadership in Greensboro, North Carolina. During this time, I was their H. Smith Richardson Jr. Visiting Fellow for 2016. Thanks in particular to John Ryan, Jennifer Martineau, and Lyndon Rego. CCL has contributed so much to my thinking over the years, and I hope that they will carry the literacies in this book to a much wider audience than I could reach alone.

The dedication for this book is to Nico, Robbie, and Everett, our three grandsons. We have one more grandchild on the way as I finish this book. Their parents Cory, Amanda, Lisa, and Zach are doing such a wonderful job of nurturing them toward the future. Each time I see them, I'm reminded about how important it is for leaders to make the future a better place for all.

Finally, I believe that coffee shops and cafés play an important part in intellectual life globally. As a writer, I seek out those cozy safe zones and feel a warm glow whenever I'm inside one. I wrote much of this book in San Mateo at Kaffeehaus. Thanks, Val!

INDEX

ABOUT THE AUTHOR

BOB JOHANSEN is a distinguished fellow at Institute for the Future in Silicon Valley. Bob is focused on writing books, as well as doing keynote talks and workshops around those books. He works with a wide range of senior leadership teams—as well as rising star leaders in executive development programs. Bob now co-leads one or two custom forecasts at a time for leaders of large organizations such as Walmart, United Rentals, Nestlé, Carnival Corporation, and Procter & Gamble.

This is Bob's tenth book, including the two editions of *Leaders Make the Future*. He was recently named the H. Smith Richardson Jr. Visiting Fellow at the Center for Creative Leadership and received the Boston University Executive Development Roundtable Marion Gislason Award for Excellence in Leadership, which recognizes "humility, generosity, and concern for others."

Bob was IFTF's president for eight years, and he created what is now called the Technology Horizons Program, which is still thriving as a way of making sense out of emerging technologies, looking ten years ahead.

A social scientist with an interdisciplinary background, Bob Johansen holds a BS degree from the University of Illinois, which he attended on a basketball scholarship, and a PhD from Northwestern University, where he arrived with a focus on sociology of religion but left with a focus on the social implications of networked connectivity. Bob also has an MDiv degree from what is now called Colgate Rochester Crozer Divinity School, where he studied world religions and social change.

Bob is married to Robin B. Johansen, an attorney practicing constitutional law. They met at the University of Illinois and live together in Silicon Valley with a golden retriever named Atticus.

ABOUT
INSTITUTE FOR THE FUTURE

Institute for the Future (IFTF) was founded in 1968 by a group of former RAND Corporation and Stanford Research Institute scientists and engineers. Bob Johansen was the first PhD-level social scientist hired by IFTF, five years after it was founded.

The Institute is located in downtown Palo Alto, in the heart of Silicon Valley and adjacent to Stanford University. It conducts ongoing foundational forecasts that focus on global commerce, technology horizons, food, the future of work, and well-being. IFTF partners with a wide range of companies and individuals for its ongoing foundational forecasts.

In addition, IFTF conducts custom forecasts that apply the foundation forecasts to a particular organization.

As it nears its 50th anniversary, IFTF is focused on developing a global literacy of the future that includes

- Convening global conversations about civic futures
- Designing and prototyping positive civic platforms
- Defining participatory methodologies for evidence-based civic futures

- Embedding IFTF's public channels in the emerging civic infrastructure
- Serving as a bridge between public and private innovators
- Creating a global network of futures education and practice

Bob does all of his talks, workshops, and custom forecasts through Institute for the Future. All of the proceeds from this book go to Institute for the Future.

For more information, visit http://www.iftf.org.

Berrett–Koehler
Publishers

Berrett-Koehler is an independent publisher dedicated to an ambitious mission: *Connecting people and ideas to create a world that works for all.*

We believe that the solutions to the world's problems will come from all of us, working at all levels: in our organizations, in our society, and in our own lives. Our BK Business books help people make their organizations more humane, democratic, diverse, and effective (we don't think there's any contradiction there). Our BK Currents books offer pathways to creating a more just, equitable, and sustainable society. Our BK Life books help people create positive change in their lives and align their personal practices with their aspirations for a better world.

All of our books are designed to bring people seeking positive change together around the ideas that empower them to see and shape the world in a new way.

And we strive to practice what we preach. At the core of our approach is Stewardship, a deep sense of responsibility to administer the company for the benefit of all of our stakeholder groups including authors, customers, employees, investors, service providers, and the communities and environment around us. Everything we do is built around this and our other key values of quality, partnership, inclusion and sustainability.

This is why we are both a B-Corporation and a California Benefit Corporation—a certification and a for-profit legal status that require us to adhere to the highest standards for corporate, social, and environmental performance.

We are grateful to our readers, authors, and other friends of the company who consider themselves to be part of the BK Community. We hope that you, too, will join us in our mission.

A BK Business Book

We hope you enjoy this BK Business book. BK Business books pioneer new leadership and management practices and socially responsible approaches to business. They are designed to provide you with groundbreaking and practical tools to transform your work and organizations while upholding the triple bottom line of people, planet, and profits. High-five!

To find out more, visit **www.bkconnection.com.**

Berrett–Koehler
Publishers

Connecting people and ideas
to create a world that works for all

Dear Reader,

Thank you for picking up this book and joining our worldwide community of Berrett-Koehler readers. We share ideas that bring positive change into people's lives, organizations, and society.

To welcome you, we'd like to offer you a free e-book. You can pick from among twelve of our bestselling books by entering the promotional code **BKP92E** here: http://www.bkconnection.com/welcome.

When you claim your free e-book, we'll also send you a copy of our e-newsletter, the *BK Communiqué*. Although you're free to unsubscribe, there are many benefits to sticking around. In every issue of our newsletter you'll find

- A free e-book
- Tips from famous authors
- Discounts on spotlight titles
- Hilarious insider publishing news
- A chance to win a prize for answering a riddle

Best of all, our readers tell us, "Your newsletter is the only one I actually read." So claim your gift today, and please stay in touch!

Sincerely,

Charlotte Ashlock
Steward of the BK Website

Questions? Comments? Contact me at bkcommunity@bkpub.com.

FSC
www.fsc.org
MIX
Paper from
responsible sources
FSC® C016245

Certified
B
Corporation
bcorporation.net